LEGENDS OF THE

UTAH

MYTHS & LEGENDS

THE TRUE STORIES BEHIND
HISTORY'S MYSTERIES

SECOND EDITION

MICHAEL O'REILLY

TWODOT®

GUILFORD, CONNECTICUT
HELENA, MONTANA

A · TWODOT® · BOOK

An imprint of Globe Pequot
An imprint and registered trademark of Rowman & Littlefield

Distributed by NATIONAL BOOK NETWORK

Copyright © 2017 Rowman & Littlefield

British Library Cataloguing-in-Publication Information available

Library of Congress Cataloging-in-Publication Data
Names: O'Reilly, Michael, author.
Title: Utah myths and legends / Michael O'Reilly.
Other titles: Mysteries and legends of Utah
Description: Second edition. | Guilford, Conn. : TwoDot, an imprint of Globe
   Pequot, 2017. | Series: The true stories behind history's mysteries |
   Includes bibliographical references and index.
Identifiers: LCCN 2017022630 (print) | LCCN 2017024011 (ebook) | ISBN
   9781493028399 | ISBN 9781493028382 (pbk.)
Subjects: LCSH: Utah—History—Anecdotes. | Utah—Biography—Anecdotes. |
   Curiosities and wonders—Utah. | Legends—Utah.
Classification: LCC F826.6 (ebook) | LCC F826.6 .O74 2017 (print) | DDC
   979.2—dc23
LC record available at https://lccn.loc.gov/2017022630

Printed in the United States of America

This book is for any adventurous spirit whose imagination is set spinning by stories of the past. And to those who have never been to Utah, but hear a gentle voice telling them, "Go West," I say do your very best to answer that call and make the Rocky Mountains your home, at least for a while.

CONTENTS

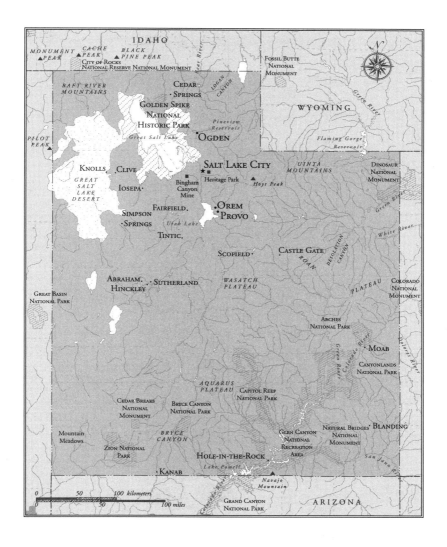

UTAH

ACKNOWLEDGMENTS

I would like to thank all of the writers and teachers I have known, especially my editor Allen Jones, a person whose advice and insight has been the most valuable part of this experience.

INTRODUCTION

U tah shares exciting pieces of American history with other parts of the West. Yet the stories told by residents of the Beehive State are as unique as the geology of Moab and as mysterious as the foggy mist cloaking the Great Salt Lake. From the tall mountains to the broad, sage-covered valleys, there are secrets waiting to be revealed to those observant enough to recognize the clues.

If while exploring a seemingly barren Utah hillside, you happened to notice a couple of old ruts in the soil, long-since grown over by prairie grass, would you picture a wagon train rolling slowly along the path some 150 years earlier? To see such things unfold in your mind is to know that you are standing *on* a piece of history and have succeeded in shrinking the gap between past and present, between the pioneers of yesterday and the skiers and mountain bikers of today.

The immediate connection with the history of land is one reason so many people are attracted to great western states like Utah, where the winds roll across vast open plains and the rugged mountains still guard the secrets of centuries past.

Stories have always been a way for cultures to pass information down through generations, and the people of Utah are no exception. Sometimes the stories most frequently told are unsolved mysteries and nearly unbelievable tales. Because we don't know the whole truth of certain events, it is these stories that undergo the most change over time, as they are told and retold around campfires, in hunting lodges, and in schoolyards.

The Mormon religion is the major element that separates Utah's people and history from that of other western states. Many stories, including a few in this book, are deeply intertwined with the mythology found in the Book of Mormon and with the men and women who brought their religion west.

Whether or not they really happened, whether or not they can ever be proven or resolved, all of the stories in this book are part of Utah's past. One thing that is definitely true is that this author did not make up these stories. They were researched and retold, and they were probably changed a little bit, the way every storyteller adds his or her own voice and inflection.

The power of myth and legend lies in the fact that good stories don't *need* to be proven or solved to be exciting or entertaining or to teach us a lesson. Some stories, like the pursuit of Rafael Lopez, seem to lose some of their attraction when they are solved. When the case is closed, we tend to put these stories away, because some of the suspense is lost. This phenomenon reveals much about our own culture and our desire to hear and talk about the unknown. So we exchange our "solved" mysteries for even older, stranger stories, as these are the ones with loose ends, yarns ready to be spun once again around the flickering glow of the campfire.

CHAPTER 1

High Desert Archaeology

As we wandered the alien topography of Utah's Canyonlands National Park, my three companions and I struggled to believe features so unique could exist anywhere in the world. Dizzy from the surreal geology unfolding before us, each vista more beautiful than the previous, we rounded a bend in the bottom of a slot canyon and froze in silent astonishment.

Affixed precariously to the side of the sandstone face, some thirty feet up, was a thousand-year-old, single-room apartment. Like hundreds of other cliff dwellings discovered throughout the Southwest, it had been carefully crafted of quarried stone pieces, stacked and buttressed by wooden support beams hewn from a juniper tree. Just as amazing was the perfectly square, window-size opening on one side, as if the builder had placed an order with the Roman Empire for a pane of glass that never arrived.

The precisely mitered architecture juxtaposed against the flowing contours of the canyon walls was enough to raise a few questions: Who built it, and when? Why would anyone choose such a remote and difficult location? Did a winged humanoid species once flutter up each night like barn swallows to their adobe domicile? At that moment, under the heat of a prehistoric star, standing in a corridor tucked into the edge of an endless desert,

I felt a scintillating and acute awareness of my place in time, on a scale of millennia rather than centuries or decades.

Our camping trip was by no means an archaeological excursion, but the next morning I found an artifact I'd like to think most amateurs looking for pottery or arrowheads wouldn't notice. We had spent the night under the stars on the flat part of a red rock formation, which continued to radiate heat after sunset, when temperatures dipped. Our sleeping bags were just a few feet from rock overhangs too shallow to call caves but deep enough to protect one from the rain. I figured someone had taken shelter there, at some point. A casual combing of the shallow sand produced no tools or pottery, but I did find a little balled-up cluster of fibers. Nesting material for a mouse, I figured. A closer inspection had me convinced they were yucca plant fibers. As I teased apart the strands, I realized they were not part of a tangle, but two frayed ends of a rope made of multiple yucca fibers. The almond-size thing in the middle of the fray was a single overhand knot, possibly tied about eight hundred years earlier.

Archaeologists know that prehistoric natives used rope ladders to enter and exit their cliff dwellings. They made their ropes out of yucca fibers, which are as strong as hemp. Had I really found a knot tied by a prehistoric human? I'm not sure, but I do know the arid climate of the Southwest is why many ancient artifacts have stood the test of time. It's possible the strongest part of a rope made from such a resilient fiber would have done the same.

Later that day, under the same ledge, I found a very small, dried section of a corncob. Perhaps an animal had raided the garbage of some campers just like me, twenty, fifty years before I was born. Then again, the ancient people of this area grew corn. In fact, archaeologists have identified the species of corn they grew. A simple DNA analysis of the specimen could have given me the answer. Alas, such information cannot be top priority for a twenty-year-old English major, and I left the corncob where I found it.

Now, two decades later, I cannot recall the route we took to access our campsite, or the ancient ruin. The unnamed cliff dwelling was not found on any Park Service map, and I have not been able to find a photograph of the exact structure I saw. Thankfully, the talented and adventurous photographer Rick Schaffer has documented many similar ruins.

There are multiple ancient cliff dwelling settlements in the Four Corners area, where the borders of Utah, Colorado, Arizona, and New Mexico join together. Some contain dozens of elevated living quarters, granaries, and even sophisticated aqueduct systems. These larger, more well-known sites include Canyon de Chelly in Arizona, New Mexico's Chaco Canyon, and Mesa Verde in Colorado.

I was impressed beyond words by what I saw a year earlier at Mesa Verde. But there was something even more special about coming across that single dwelling, in the middle of nowhere, with a few of my friends. For one thing, there was no parking lot. No gift shop. No asphalt path leading to observation points, benches, or drinking fountains. We came upon the spot more or less exactly as it looked when its inhabitants walked away from it some seven hundred years earlier.

The archaeological name for the people who built the cliff dwellings in the Four Corners area, "Anasazi," is a Navajo word meaning "ancient enemy." It was appropriated by archaeologists needing a catch-all term for a diverse culture whose structure and traditions weren't—and still aren't—fully understood.

The Anasazi are known for their cliff dwellings but, interestingly, they only occupied these structures for about two hundred years before abandoning them for unknown reasons in the fourteenth century. Over the course of centuries prior, habitation structures evolved from shallow, circular pithouses to small kivas, then to "roomblocks" and larger kivas, some of which were used only for ceremonial purposes.

The Anasazi were not a single culture, but were composed of at least four other ancient peoples: the Hohokam, Sinagua, and Salado peoples, who were centered in present-day Arizona; and the Mogollon people, who moved north from Mexico to settle in an area spanning central Arizona and New Mexico.

In the 1930s Harold Gladwin, a New York stockbroker-turned-archaeologist, moved to Arizona and developed a "root and stem" taxonomy to make sense of the way indigenous peoples of the Southwest merged with and evolved into groups of historical record. This system of classification has been expanded over the years, culminating in the widely accepted theory that the Anasazi eventually became modern Pueblos.

The main question vexing archaeologists since Gladwin's day has been why the Anasazi left their homes so abruptly, around AD 1300. For many years, the most popular explanation centered on a major drought that spanned the last quarter of the thirteenth century and likely prompted the Anasazi to vacate the Four Corners region. Over the last several decades, however, evidence against that

The Honeycomb Ruin is just one example of the hundreds of man-made cliff dwellings found throughout the American Southwest.
RICH SHAFER

theory has mounted. Multiple studies of ancient tree-ring growth has revealed other droughts of similar severity, all of which the Anasazi managed to live through. Some have pointed to increasing population levels that may have put stress on local resources and out-stripped the region's carrying capacity, triggering a mass migration.

Another critical thing scientists cannot agree on is the social/political structure of the Anasazi. This lack of context is a major detriment when trying to theorize about the decision-making process of an ancient population. Some believe the Anasazi lived an egalitarian existence, in which various responsibilities were shared by all, as were the spoils of a successful hunt or the annual crop harvest. Others have suggested a system of hierarchy, with a ruling class of elites who called the shots.

Archaeology may never provide answers to questions about Anasazi social structure. Perhaps, as University of Denver professor Dean Saitta believes, they aren't the right questions to ask. Saitta and others have proposed the Anasazi were composed of multiple cultural groups that chose to live in a location that had a common spiritual and/or practical value. In this scenario the Anasazi successfully embraced diversity in the same way most modern civilizations have. Eventually, however, some set of circumstances led to the collapse of their social structure and/or prevented the establishment of a system for managing the complex dynamics of a growing population.

Saitta's research supports earlier theories suggesting that, regardless of their abrupt departure, the Anasazi did not simply vanish but instead integrated into Rio Grande Pueblo, Hopi, and Zuni tribal bloodlines, eventually becoming the modern Pueblos. For this reason, Pueblos understandably prefer the term "Ancestral Puebloan" over "Anasazi," the latter being associated for so long with a disappeared culture. Archaeologists, however, continue to use "Anasazi," not in an ethnographical context but in a chronological and geographical one.

Mesmerized by Anasazi lore, I set out to write an entire chapter about them. At some point during my deep entanglement in jargon-filled dissertations on DNA procedures and reports of academic disagreements fierce enough to spark tweed-shredding archaeo-lectual brawls on campuses across the Southwest, I began to feel the Anasazi were not as mysterious as I'd been led to believe. Although many of the details were still up for grabs, the logical conclusions about the Anasazi's fate had transformed some of their mythology into hard fact. A bit of my intrigue for the unknown had been brushed away like dust from an ancient pottery shard.

In one sense, the story of the Anasazi—never actually a singular cultural or ethnic group—has taken on the flavor of a cultural marketing campaign, an unintentional branding of a mythological construct. I don't say that to downplay the importance of their existence, nor to suggest things were fabricated to make the Anasazi appear more interesting. Rather, what is most interesting about them is what we don't know.

Scientists and armchair archaeologists still quibble over the precise reason the Anasazi abandoned the Four Corners. Even if they do reach a consensus on that point, the news won't be nearly as exciting as the original story, which reads like a Hollywood elevator pitch waiting for a screenplay: A group of people with no written language but incredible knowledge of architecture, astronomy, and agriculture thrives for millennia before spontaneously disappearing into the desert.

An epic blockbuster about the lost Anasazi may never be made. The Ancestral Puebloans, however, will likely remain the darlings of Southwest prehistory not because of who they were or how they disappeared, but for the photogenic architectural wonders they left behind.

Researchers relied mainly on archeological and linguistic data and only scant DNA evidence to draw a reasonably clear picture of what became of the Anasazi. Ironically, more extensive DNA testing has done exactly the opposite for another prehistoric people, the Fremont, about whom archaeologists currently have more questions than answers.

Most of Utah is encompassed by the eastern edge of the Great Basin, a unique area of the American West from which no waterway flows out to an ocean. Instead, rivers run into lakes or dissipate into marshes, where the water slowly evaporates or sinks into the soil.

Utah's ancient Fremont people, who occupied the "desert mountain island" for a thousand years, were one of the only prehistoric groups in North America that remain genetically isolated from any modern population. When we search for clues about the Fremont, we learn more about who they were and how they lived than what became of them. Instead of spreading their descendants along migratory corridors and settlements across the land, the Fremont were much like the water of the Great Basin, their story a tale of containment, absorption, and evaporation.

In 1931, while excavating a site along the Fremont River in south-central Utah, archaeologist Noel Morss found evidence of a culture similar to the Anasazi, yet different in several ways. Hedging his bets, he labeled his find "Puebloid," to imply a simultaneous similarity to and distinction from the Anasazi. Others suspected the Fremont were very different from the Anasazi, based on artifacts alone.

While the Anasazi were expert weavers of natural fibers, creating rope, sandals, and other garments, they never mastered the art of fine leatherwork. The Fremont, on the other hand, wore moccasins made from the hocks of mountain sheep and deer. And although the Fremont also were adept at the craft of basketry, their baskets were notably different from the Anasazi's both in design and material. Even the pictographs and petroglyphs the Fremont left on rock faces in the Great Basin are distinct from the artwork created by their neighbors to the southeast.

Then there's the pottery. Ancient civilizations around the world made clay vessels for everyday use. Thousands of years later, those same ceramic pots—even when broken—can hold clues about who made them. Shapes, decoration, and production techniques change across time, and from culture to culture. The clay artifacts found at Fremont sites seem to have been made by hands unfamiliar with the techniques and style of the Anasazi.

It was Morss who first defined the Fremont as a culture, but he proposed they were a northern offshoot of the Anasazi. Within a few years another researcher, Julian Steward, suggested a cluster of sites north of the Great Salt Lake be included as part of the Fremont complex.

By the 1950s consensus had been reached on the designation of five regional Fremont variants, or subcultures: Sevier, Great Salt Lake, Parawan, Uinta, and San Rafael. This classification was helpful, but there remained plenty of distinction between the groups from an archaeological standpoint. By the 1960s arguments over both the origins of the Fremont and their fate had become more contentious than any debate over the Anasazi. Notable researcher Melvin Aikens believed the Fremont descended from a specific, southward migration of ancient Athabaskans. University of Nebraska archaeologist James Gunnerson proposed, following Morss, that the Fremont were a branch of the Anasazi, cast off north and west. Eventually, Gunnerson theorized, the Fremont merged with the Numic-speaking Shoshone and Ute peoples, who had moved into the area from the south around AD 500.

In the late nineties, DNA tests were conducted on forty-seven Fremont skeletons found north of the Great Salt Lake, their ages spanning two archaeological phases, from AD 400 to 1350. The results showed just how different the Fremont were, not only from the Anasazi but from everyone else. Researchers analyzed bone fragments, looking for genetic markers, or "haplogroups" (A, B, C, and D), found in all modern-day Native Americans. These four distinct gene variations emerged on North American soil during three or four major migration waves that occurred just before and during the end of the last ice age, 30,000 to 15,000 years ago.

The people who had made their way northeast from Asia (and everywhere else in the East) eventually reached a dry land bridge called "Beringia," which spanned the present-day Bering Strait between Russia and Alaska. It was from this location that multiple groups—over different periods, spanning millennia—descended south into North America, bringing with them the five haplogroups that would come to define the ancestry of all native people on both American continents, or "Amerinds." (Haplogroup X was not measured in this study, as it is found in northeastern populations.)

By measuring the frequency at which the markers occur within the genetic code sequence, the researchers could come closer in determining where the Fremont came from, and what became of them. They were surprised when they noticed the absence of haplogroup A, which appears at a consistently high rate in North Amerinds. This finding refuted Aikens's Athabaskan origin theory. In addition, haplogroup B was measured at a much higher frequency than it occurs in the Shoshone who, Gunnerson and others had theorized, had merged with and replaced the Fremont. Archaeologist Albert Schroeder countered Gunnerson's assessment in 1963, arguing that, right up until the fourteenth century, the differences between Shoshone and Fremont artifacts suggest an overlap rather than an outright displacement of the Fremont by the Shoshone. The implication is that, although the Fremont were widely dispersed across the Great Basin contemporaneously with other prehistoric populations, their genetic fingerprint seems to have disappeared by the fifteenth century.

A 1998 essay by David Madsen and Steven Simms reveals the first coherent picture of Fremont agriculture practices and their sporadic shifts between subsistence strategies. Madsen offers four specific date ranges for the cessation of farming practices at different locations, beginning with the Uinta Basin, around AD 1000. Farming stopped in the Parowan Valley and Great Salt Lake wetlands between 1100 and 1150. Sometime between 1250 and 1300, coinciding with a twenty-five-year drought, it appears that agriculture came to a standstill across most of the Great Basin. It's believed the Fremont sites in northwest Colorado put down their farm tools, for good, around 1450.

The "prehistory" of the Americas begins later than it does in many areas of the world. By the time the Anasazi and Fremont were figuring out the bow and arrow, for example, the Chinese had been holding archery tournaments for millennia. In the context of other civilizations, AD 1300 doesn't seem that long ago. When trying to understand a culture that had no written language, however, it seems almost as easy to hypothesize about some dinosaur's favorite color. Of course, we must not confuse a lack of writing with dim-wittedness. Both the Fremont and the Anasazi possessed not only immense technical skill and dexterity, but detailed knowledge of a vast geographical area and the resources it held. Both were farmers of corn and other crops. The Fremont's most valuable asset was their adaptability, as evidenced by the five regional variant groups thriving across a wide range of environments. They adjusted their lifestyles according to social and ecological factors, vacillating for centuries between a farming culture and a nomadic, hunting/ gathering culture. Archaeological evidence suggests the Fremont were immensely creative and resourceful, using a wide range of survival strategies.

The circumstances that forced the Ancestral Puebloans from their brick apartments in the cliffs may never be fully understood, just as we may never get a grasp on who the Fremont people became. Our imaginations are guided in the other direction anyway. Archaeology may have provided us with a picture of how the Fremont spent their days in Utah over a period of five hundred to a thousand years, but genetic anthropologists have coaxed from their ancient bones a tale that spans fifteen thousand years.

CHAPTER 2

Jedediah Smith: Tough Trapper, Shrewd Businessman, Explorer Extraordinaire

Jedediah Smith took no pleasure in killing his horse. Not just because it was a perfectly good animal, besides being skinny and dehydrated. No, he was so hungry he would have killed the horse he was riding if it wouldn't leave him stranded. But the men needed food, there was one packhorse left, and the Great Salt Lake was not yet even a mirage on the distant horizon.

After a rough west-to-east crossing of California's Sierra Nevada mountains, Smith and two companions, Robert Evans and Silas Gobel, had been forced to kill three of their pack animals, as wild game became scarce. They went for days at a time without water until finally they hit the Utah border. Upon seeing the vast Great Basin before them, they prayed to God that the meat of one skinny mare would sufficiently nourish them and that they would survive the torturous, searing heat of the same God's desert sun.

With a single gunshot the deed was done, and the men cut the horse meat into strips, allowing it to dry. Continuing northeast, along what is now called Thomas Creek, near the Deep Creek Mountains, Smith saw a group of antelope, but he could not get a shot with his rifle. He did manage, however, to kill a couple of hares that the men savored, knowing the land ahead would be barren.

A few days later Jedediah climbed a small mountain and saw nothing but another vast, dry valley and a small mountain range (the Stansburys) to the northeast, about sixty miles away. Had he a good pair of binoculars, Smith may have seen the Great Salt Lake just beyond the mountains, but after seeing nothing of great promise, he climbed down and returned, dejectedly, to the other men.

He was the most honest of any mountain man in the West, but even Jedediah knew when to tell a lie. To keep their hopes alive, he told Evans and Gobel that there was a dark spot in the distance, probably a spring. They set out at a moderate pace, stopping occasionally to rest under what little shade they found, digging down to cool sand and lying in the shallow graves for a spell.

On June 25, without an ounce of strength to continue, Evans lay down under the scant shade of a cedar tree and told Smith and Gobel to go on without him. For Smith the decision was not a tough one, but it was not one he wanted to make. Unless he and Gobel went on for help, there would be no hope for any of the three.

After leaving Evans on his own, Smith and Gobel continued north through the Skull Valley, where they saw two Indians in the distance. They were headed in Evans's direction. A short time later Smith heard gunshots and presumed their partner to be dead. Luckily Smith came across a spring later that afternoon, and after quenching his own thirst, he filled a kettle and headed back to Evans. The Indians had not killed him after all, and Evans's strength was restored in short order.

As they followed the Stansbury Range north, the group encountered a few Indians who kindly provided some antelope meat and told them they were close to buffalo country. The next day Smith climbed to a point where he could see the Great Salt Lake, and he was delighted to be near one of his favorite western locations. In his journal he commented on his affinity for Utah and mentioned that the Salt Lake Valley "had become my home of the wilderness."

Smith was encouraged to be in familiar territory again, but he knew better than to think he was home free. The natural elements of the outdoors have a way of killing a tired, malnourished man who doesn't have his wits about him. The party was at least a week away from the 1827 Mountain Man Rendezvous at Bear Lake, and there would be no relaxing until they arrived.

Two days later the men were tested by the rushing Jordan River. There were no easy options for crossing the vicious torrent, and the spot they chose was sixty yards, bank to bank. Evans and Gobel couldn't swim, but they did their best. Almost instantly after wading in, they were at the mercy of the current, which carried them half a mile downstream.

Smith tied himself to a makeshift raft, but became entangled in the rope as he struggled to reach the opposite bank. But he didn't come this far to get drowned in a lousy river, and, struggling with all his might, he got himself and his gear across, gathered his men, and continued north.

Smith had not necessarily been looking to become the first white man to make the west-to-east crossing from California to Salt Lake Valley, but he had no other choice. Important business awaited him at the annual Mountain Man Rendezvous.

When the three sunburned, emaciated men finally reached Bear Lake on July 3, Smith had accomplished one of several historical feats in his young life. He was a humble man, however, and he wasn't preoccupied with putting feathers in his hat. He simply went where he needed to go. A trapper first, explorer second, it was the pursuit of high-quality beaver pelts that took him to areas where no other white man had ever been.

Most people imagine Smith as a self-reliant woodsman—a rough, weather-beaten man dressed in buckskin, stinking of beaver musk and toting a musket and a few rusty traps. While this image may be somewhat accurate, it is one perpetuated by popular western mythology and gives us only a glimpse of Jedediah Smith, the *character*.

What made Jedediah Smith, the *man*, interesting were the things that separated him from other trappers and frontiersmen. Along with his taste for adventure and a passion for the outdoors, Smith was business savvy, and by age thirty he had become a fur-industry baron. He was not only the leader of his own company but an ambassador to various Indian tribes, many of whom had never encountered whites. With his diplomatic voice and gentle tone, Smith always seemed to win the friendship of natives, regardless of any language barrier.

Born in New York, Smith was never content with simply observing nature. He spent his youth as an active participant, traipsing through hardwood forests in pursuit of squirrels and rabbits. His choice of careers was a continuation of his energetic childhood. The beaver became his livelihood, the elk his food, the deer his clothing, the buffalo his sleeping bag.

Smith knew how to suffer in the wilderness, without food or water, without complaining, without panicking. And he did it all without maps, as we have them today, and without any solid knowledge of what dangers or opportunities lay beyond the next mountain range.

The virtue of self-sufficiency was important to Smith, but so was his spirituality. It was his faith in God, and a belief in Divine Providence, that got him through the hard times and guided him through the toughest decisions.

By the time the Smith family found themselves in northern Illinois, in 1822, St. Louis, Missouri, had become a boomtown and commercial hub of the western US and Canadian fur companies. It was here that Smith's life as a hunter and trapper began in earnest, with an unusual call for "enterprising young men," in the *St. Louis Enquirer*.

The man responsible for the ad, which ran in several papers between mid-February and late March, was General William Ashley of the Missouri Fur Company. The expedition up the Missouri River "to its source" promised an unspecified form of employment for up to three years. Smith was intrigued by the vague offer. Ever since reading of the Lewis and Clark expedition, he had dreamed of adventure in the unknown West. Finally he had the chance to do it.

After inquiring about the offer, Smith was assigned to follow Major Andrew Henry's detachment of twenty-one men up the Missouri River. Smith's job was to provide food for the expedition, and he did so by killing deer and antelope, as well as a variety of small game. The summer and autumn journey took them northwest, almost as far as Great Falls, Montana, and then they spent a cold winter on the Musselshell River.

The following May, Henry was faced with a major obstacle in the form of the Rocky Mountains. He decided the only practical way to get through the Yellowstone area was on horse-back. Although local bands of Sioux, Crow, and Arikara Indians had horses, trading with them had been difficult in the past, so Henry attempted to get a message downstream to General Ashley, requesting that Ashley obtain some sturdy mounts. In the first of many acts of bravery and duty, Smith volunteered to make the trip, and he set out with a small group of others.

On May 30 Smith encountered Ashley's group near an encampment of Arikara Indians, just as Ashley had arrived there. The "Rees" had a reputation for being unpredictable, and recent battles with whites had left them edgy. Ashley offered gifts to the two chiefs and tried to assure them that his group came in peace and wanted to trade for horses. The chiefs listened, but they would not admit the whites into their camp, where proud warriors milled about, vastly outnumbering Ashley's ninety or so.

The Ree elders retreated to discuss whether or not they should even let the whites pass unharmed, while Ashley and his men waited nervously on their boats in the middle of the river. Finally the Rees agreed to put aside any negative feelings and offered to do some trading the next day. Ashley felt more relaxed about the situation now and was encouraged by the Ree's promise of forty or fifty horses and some buffalo robes.

The following morning Ashley purchased nineteen horses and some other items. But when the Rees wanted guns and ammu-nition, Ashley's men refused, and all trading came to halt. The infuriated Indians once again retreated to council. Ashley later accepted an invitation to Chief Bear's tent, where he was told in no uncertain terms his party would be attacked the following day. He was even advised to swim across the river in order to escape. Ashley returned to his boat with a sick feeling in his stomach. He wasn't so sure the Rees really wanted him to get away.

Shortly after midnight, shouting was heard among the Indians, and moments later news came that a white man, Aaron Stephens, had been killed. All of Ashley's men were rousted and called to arm themselves. Around daybreak a Ree came forward to offer the body of Stephens in exchange for a horse. Tension rose with the prolonged deliberation over the exchange of the horse when someone claimed that Stephens's body had been mutilated. Ashley's men were outraged, but still outnumbered.

Amid the confusion and chaos, Jedediah tried to size up the situation. He was willing to fight for the men he was with, but there's no doubt he must have had a bitter taste about his luck and timing: to arrive in camp just in time for an Indian attack.

As the sun broke over the horizon, Smith looked toward the lower Ree camp and observed a strange sight. For a second or two, it appeared as if the camp had blossomed with giant, fluffy white flowers. But just as he heard the muffled reports of exploding black powder, the little lead musket balls were whistling past him, slamming through boat hulls.

A few men returned fire immediately, but those caught out in the open were wounded or killed. Others scrambled to escape the melee, ignoring Ashley's orders to fight back. Smith was one of a handful of cool heads who found cover behind a couple of wounded horses. Yet their position was not good; they were exposed out on the beach, pinned down by gunfire.

One by one each man on the beach made a dash for the river, frantically swimming for the far bank, as lead balls tore through the water around him. Some made it, some did not. Finally it was Smith's turn, and, after firing one last shot at the Rees, he tucked his rifle into his belt and sprinted for the water. The current carried him past the splashing rain of gunfire, and he made it safely downstream. Later that day he reunited with Ashley, hearing the news that fourteen men had died in the attack and nine others were wounded.

It was the first time Smith had met Ashley, his boss and future business partner, and Smith's bravery during the fight did not go unnoticed by Ashley. The general had a feeling Smith could be relied on, and it was confirmed when Smith volunteered to deliver the news of the attack back to Henry's party.

Smith and a French Canadian departed for the Yellowstone area, and when they arrived, Smith was made captain of a company of fighters called the Missouri Legion, organized to fight the Rees. As he continued to prove his leadership abilities, Smith was appointed, by Ashley, to head an exploration west, through the Badlands and Black Hills, in search of beaver.

Smith spent the next year learning about the West, the native tribes of the mountains, and the ins and outs of the fur industry. If what he had already experienced was typical of the trapper's life, he was sure to encounter more danger along his path. Still he couldn't help but fall in love with the sights, the freedom, and the opportunity of the vast American wilderness.

The next big opportunity presented itself to Smith in the fall of 1825, when Major Henry decided he wanted out of the partnership with Ashley. Smith had accompanied Ashley to St. Louis, where they unloaded around $50,000 in beaver pelts, accumulated by all the trappers of the Missouri Fur Company. Ashley was eager to send another expedition west, before winter set in, and he knew Smith was the right man to lead the group.

Less than a month later, Smith was off to the Rockies again, this time with seventy men, 160 horses, and some $20,000 in supplies and trading goods. Now he was not just working for the Missouri Fur Company, he was representing the firm as Ashley's new business partner.

Smith took his men south of Wyoming's Teton Mountains, to the Salt Lake Valley, where they spent the winter. The following spring a trapping excursion took Smith north, into Idaho, before returning back to Bear Lake, where he met up with other trappers at the 1826 Mountain Man Rendezvous. The annual event was held in late summer so that fur trappers could sell their pelts and stock up on supplies for the next season. That year Ashley sold his share of the Missouri Fur Company to Smith for around $5,000, and two other men stepped in to form the trading firm Smith, Jackson, and Sublett.

Smith's goal for his next expedition, departing the Rendezvous in August, was to find out whether or not a mythical river called the Buenaventura actually existed. Some claimed that the Great Salt Lake fed the uncharted river, which made its way all the way to the Pacific Ocean. Although no white man had ever explored the area, Smith envisioned the Buenaventura coursing through virgin territory, holding untold numbers of high-grade beaver.

The previous spring, Smith had investigated the northwestern shores of the Salt Lake and found no river outlet, so he decided to take his group southwest in hopes of finding the Buenaventura. But Smith's optimism was always tempered with caution, and he was humbled as he set out with his fifteen men toward the rocky, treeless desert. This was the *real* uncharted West, and this would be the trip that would determine what the young leader was made of.

As they made their way south, through Utah Valley, the group encountered Ute Indians who had not been visited by foreigners since the Spaniards Escalante and Dominguez came, bearing crosses and the news of Jesus, in 1776. To show his peaceful intentions, Smith provided the Utes with gifts of knives, tobacco, and gunpowder. The Utes, however, were of little help in describing the land south and west of Utah Lake.

The trappers followed the Sevier River (named "Ashley's River" by Smith) for about seventy miles, but they were forced to abandon its course when steep canyon walls closed around the banks. Smith knew he was not in beaver country. The high desert, with its stunted cedars and junipers and endless miles of sagebrush, was not the right climate or habitat for the large, toothy water rodents.

On October 4, Smith crossed the Colorado River and followed it for another month before reaching the desolate and dangerous Mojave Desert. Of course they had spent months in the desert already, and perhaps their utter innocence of the territory actually helped them, for accurate knowledge of the challenge that lay before them would have weighed heavily on their minds. On November 26, Smith's group reached the fertile San Bernardino Valley and the Pacific Ocean. They were now in territory still ruled by the Spanish, and they were careful not to upset the local authorities.

After two weeks of lazing around the bountiful orchards of the Spanish missions, enjoying the mild weather, Smith had a meeting with Governor-General Jose Maria Echeandia. The governor did not seem to understand the act of beaver trapping, and he showed a fair amount of suspicion toward Smith and his men. The resourceful Smith was able to find a shipmaster in San Diego, however, who took a look at Smith's fur-trading papers and convinced Echeandia that the whites meant no harm. Echeandia was put at ease and decided to allow Smith's group to pass through, but they were forbidden from going north, up the coast. Smith agreed not to go up the coast and instead went inland, before turning north along the Sierra Nevada mountains, traveling until early May.

With no way around the massive mountain range, Smith chose a rushing torrent now known as the American River to follow into the Sierras, hoping it would lead to the mythical Buenaventura. They had succeeded in their quest to find beaver, and as they grunted through the foothills, toward the granite teeth of the Sierras, their horses toted some 1,500 pounds of pelts. Smith realized his load was too big and his men too many for an efficient mountain crossing, especially if he wanted to make the Rendezvous by July. Leaving the majority of the party behind with the beaver pelts, Smith took Evans and Gobel and headed up into the mountains, promising the others he would return in four months.

Smith's crossing of the Sierras was another first, and he had done it in only eight days, losing two horses and a mule along the way. No other white man had made the trip from the west, from California through Nevada. Finally, the tired and hungry trio found themselves back in Utah, where we encountered them at the beginning of our story.

Smith's year-long trip had done a lot for establishing him as a successful trapper, businessman, and diplomat. Yet even with several "first routes" to his credit, his role as an explorer was just beginning.

In the fall of 1828, Smith set off on another expedition, taking the same southwestern route out of Utah, to California. This time, instead of heading east through the Sierras again, he took his expedition north along the coast, past the Columbia River, nearly to Canada. The loop was much bigger than the previous expedition and proved to be very profitable.

A few years later, after bringing a great load of beaver pelts to market in St. Louis, Smith once again stocked up on supplies and headed west. The terrain was not particularly rough, following the Santa Fe Trail to the Arkansas River, but it was a new route for Smith, and he knew they would be traveling through hostile territory.

Smith had always managed to make peace with different tribes, but each encounter was different, and required caution. At some point, Smith's group had turned south, away from the river, and by May 27, 1831, they had endured several days without water. Smith and two others searched for a spring, but when they had no luck, Smith suggested the two others wait for him while he investigated a potential water source several miles in the distance.

As he approached the water hole, Smith noticed a small band of Comanches hiding among the rocks and sparse trees, apparently lying in wait for buffalo. By the time he realized he had stumbled upon them, he was practically surrounded by the well-camouflaged hunters. So he did what he had done many other times, and rode up to one of the men to introduce himself.

The language barrier was the least of his problems, as Smith quickly realized the Comanches did not want to be friends. Sensing the tension, and noticing others encircling him from behind, Smith spun his horse around and tried to escape. He made it only a few yards before a musket ball ripped through his left shoulder. With his good arm he discharged a shot, killing a Comanche. But before he could reach for his pistols, Smith was hit by several additional shots, which were fatal.

After searching for Smith for some time, his party went on without him. The story of his death was related by American Indians who came forward later with Smith's pistols and rifle.

Jedediah Smith explored more of the western United States than any other white man during the 1820s.
SMITH/BACON FAMILY COLLECTION, HOLT-ATHERTON
SPECIAL COLLECTIONS, UNIVERSITY OF THE PACIFIC LIBRARY

The importance of Jedediah Smith's travels have generally been overlooked by historians, who tend to revere the earlier explorations of Lewis and Clark. Yet the fact remains that, by 1830, Smith had laid eyes on more of western America than any other white man. In doing so, he opened up travel routes for countless others to follow.

Jedediah Smith was truly one of a kind, for no other mountain man had the same combination of woodsmanship, intellect, and entrepreneurial spirit. Most important, he showed the country that the American Dream could be found in the uncharted lands west of the Mississippi, if one was willing to work for it.

CHAPTER 3

The Lost Rhoades Gold Mine and the Secret of Carre Shinob

In early May 1855, a string of pack mules and horses zigzagged its way up one of the steep Uinta Mountains. Seen from a distance, there was nothing strange about it. But from the view of nineteen-year-old Caleb Rhoades, it was a macabre procession of frozen human and animal corpses.

The Ute Indians were on their way to a sacred burial site for the internment of Chief Walker, and Rhoades had been asked to come along in place of his ill father, Thomas. Caleb had felt uneasy about the trip, ever since Chiefs Arapeen and Tabiyuna, or "Tabby," had led Caleb and a small group of Indians to a temporary tomb holding Walker's frozen body. It wasn't the sight of Walker that shocked Caleb, but the bodies of two children belonging to Walker, along with two wives and some horses—all killed to accompany the Chief in the afterlife.

Besides Caleb the only other white man was Isaac Morley, a close friend of Chief Walker, and the man responsible for Walker's conversion to Mormonism. Morley felt a lump in his throat as he remembered Walker saying he would like to have a couple of Mormons buried beside him. After seeing what the Chief did to his own wives and children, what might be in store for him and young Caleb?

With their legs burning and lungs gasping on thin mountain air, they hiked for two hours before the morbid caravan suddenly came to a stop. Caleb looked around. Surely this impossibly steep, rocky hillside was not the site of the legendary ancestral burial ground known as "Carre Shinob," or "There Dwells the Great Spirit." Caleb watched two Utes walk over to a pile of boulders the size of bookcases and begin pulling them away from the side of the mountain. Gradually a cave's entrance was revealed.

The Utes solemnly carried Chief Walker and the other bodies inside. They were followed by Caleb and Morley, who had never been so nervous at a funeral. Once in the spacious cavern, Caleb was stunned by the brightness given off by just a few lanterns. Then he realized what he was looking at. The walls shimmered with the metallic brilliance of pure gold!

Not wanting to act overly excited, given the circumstances, Caleb kept his amazement to himself while trying to take in the scene. As discretely as he could, he peered around several massive stone pillars and was startled by the sight of two partially mummified bodies, each adorned with ceremonial gold and jewels. These were the bodies of Chief Walker's great-grandfather, Uin-pah-quint, and grandfather, Pana-a-pitch, or "San Pete."

Caleb spotted stacks of gold and silver bars and several wooden boxes filled with precious stones. Judging by the echo of the chanting Indians, Caleb figured there were many other caverns adjoining the room they were in.

As far back as the lanterns cast their dusty glow, he could see more skeletons, some wearing ancient Spanish armor, their leather pouches and knife sheaths still perfectly intact. There were two large, golden disks, taller than a man, each one engraved with words of a language Caleb had never seen. He couldn't fathom their value. Skeletons were adorned with elaborate feathers, jewels, and gold artifacts he did not recognize. He had a thousand questions. Could these golden disks, strange masks, anklets, and breastplates belong to the Lamanite people, written about in the *Book of Mormon*? Young Caleb only hoped he lived long enough to find out the answers.

Walker's body was fixed in a seated position and decorated with similar golden rings, necklaces, and a mask Caleb took to be of Lamanite origin. As two Utes arranged the corpses of Walker's wives and two children beside him, Caleb and Morley exchanged nervous glances.

Suddenly the voice of Chief Arapeen boomed out, "Caleb Rhoades!"

Morley's heart stopped, and Caleb's raced out of control. *This is it for us! They're getting ready to give Walker the two Mormons he wanted!*

"Yes, sir?" Caleb responded, sheepishly.

"Your father is a good man," the chief continued. "If you are like him, I can trust you. You must carry out the wishes of Brother Walker and take the gold from the Sacred Mine to give to the Church."

Caleb hardly expected to be appointed to such a task, but he preferred the job over joining Chief Walker in the afterlife. Morley and Caleb followed the chief out of the cave and into the afternoon sun, where a couple of Utes were assigned to escort Caleb to the nearby sacred mine. Chief Arapeen then turned to Morley and told him, "Do not come back to this place." And Morley never did.

The Utes knew there was value in gold, but after seeing the greed and destruction that came along with mining, they avoided the industry and often sealed up and hid old Spanish workings. Ever since Chief Walker had converted to Mormonism, however, he had been willing to help out the Church in any way he could.

Chief Walker had asked Brigham Young, future president of the Mormon Church, to find someone trustworthy, with a good knowledge of mining. Young called on Thomas Rhoades, the very same man who had returned from California three years earlier with more pure gold than any individual had ever provided for the Church. Thomas accepted the task of taking gold from the Sacred Mine, which was offered under the conditions that he would never reveal the location and that the gold would be used only for the Mormon Church.

Thomas had done a good job of keeping the mine a secret, even from Caleb, who never knew exactly where his father was going when he occasionally disappeared into the mountains. Beginning in the early 1850s he reportedly made several trips, during which he hauled out some sixty pounds of gold each time.

To be clear, the Lost Rhoades Mine, or "Sacred Mine," is not the same as the nearby ancestral burial site Carre Shinob. Both places contain vast treasure, but it was the Sacred Mine, previously worked by the Spaniards, from which Caleb and his father reportedly took their gold for the Church.

Arapeen, the new chief, was reluctant to renew the Mormons' access to the Sacred Mine because of recent tensions between the Utes and the whites. The chief was, in fact, on the verge of waging all-out war on the Mormons, claiming they had mistreated his people. Then Arapeen had a vision in which Walker urged him to help the Mormons rather than fight them. Arapeen put his grudges aside and agreed to continue to allow the Mormons into the mine, but with one stipulation. Thomas Rhoades had the assistance of several white men on most of his trips. From now on, however, Caleb would be the only white man allowed near the Sacred Mine.

Thomas Rhoades, faithful Mormon and holder of secrets
UTAH HISTORICAL SOCIETY

Worked by the Spaniards in the 1700s, the Sacred Mine was believed to hold more gold than any mine on Earth and became the most sought-after treasure in Utah. Once the area was officially declared an American Indian reservation, however, it was off-limits to prospectors.

There is no record of exactly how much gold was extracted by Caleb over the next few years, nor do we know how many trips he made. One thing we do know is that the Mormon Church was in desperate need of money.

At a time when other western states were enjoying economic expansion, Utah was financially isolated from the venture capitalists and financial institutions of the East. Money never circulated for long in Salt Lake City, because it had to be spent in California, or on the East Coast, to buy basic goods. To address this concern, a mint was even built in Salt Lake City, where thousands of gold coins were struck, in five- and ten-dollar denominations. The story of this mint and the coins produced is interesting in its own right. People still, to this day, occasionally find these Mormon coins buried in flower beds or stashed behind walls of old Salt Lake City homes.

According to Rhoades family legend, the statue of the angel Moroni, high atop the Mormon Temple in Salt Lake, was overlaid with gold from the Sacred Mine. The Church, however, has never acknowledged the origin of Moroni's gold, nor has it confirmed the existence of the mine.

By the time Chief Arapeen died in 1869, tensions between whites and Utes had worsened. Fed up with the Church's insatiable desire for gold, the new chief, Tabby, decided not to renew the gold pact with Caleb. He no longer had legal access to the Ute reservation.

For the next couple of decades, Caleb forgot about the Sacred Mine but kept a hand in the gold-prospecting game. He struck pay dirt at several claims around Utah, becoming one of the richest Mormons and, like his father, a generous contributor to the Church.

Then in 1896, Caleb made plans to negotiate another pact between his mining operation and the Utes. He decided to partner with a man named F. W. C. Hathenbruck, who promised Rhoades a one-twentieth share in any profits.

Gold mining had always been competitive, attracting the seediest of characters, but the West had gotten even wilder since Caleb had been a boy. Any man undertaking a search for the Lost

Rhoades Mines had to be good with a pick and shovel but even better with a six-shooter.

Once word got out that Rhoades was attempting to get a new lease with the Utes, several other groups of eager men assembled to beat Rhoades to the punch. One man, a mining engineer named Jesse Knight, decided he also wanted to explore the same area, near Vernal. Caleb didn't trust Knight and had a feeling he was after the Sacred Mine. Chances were that Knight didn't have a map, which meant he might try something crazy.

After getting the support of several investors from the Florence and Raven Mining Companies, Knight went to work assembling a crew of shady outlaws and thugs to make sure he got his claim—and protected it. By August, gunmen and ruffians of every stripe had gathered in Vernal, hoping to find some type of security work for one of the two competing miners. The stage was set for a true western showdown.

Caleb found his own backup protection in a man named W. E. Christiansen, also known as Matt Warner, a bank robber born in Levan, Utah. Warner had connections to the Utes, which was exactly what Caleb needed, since relations with the tribe had soured. Caleb hired two more rough characters named Bob Swift and Henry Coleman, both with experience in mining and shootouts. Swift and Warner had ties to Butch Cassidy's Wild Bunch, which frequented hideouts near the Wyoming-Utah border.

One morning in late August, Caleb sent Coleman and Swift up to a location in Dry Fork to stake claims and protect the area. A couple hours into their trip, they realized they were being followed by some of Knight's men. Under the cover of darkness, Swift took off on his horse and headed for Vernal, where he notified Warner.

Honoring his agreement to protect Caleb's interests, Warner got one more man, Bill Wall, and headed back up to confront Knight's men. They traveled all night, and by sunrise they were approaching the camp where Swift had left Coleman alone. As Warner and Wall got into a clearing near Coleman's tent, they were startled by an explosion of gunfire. Warner jumped from his horse in a flash, pulling his rifle from its scabbard and yanking Wall to the ground in the process. The two hid behind some aspen trees, while Warner returned fire on the hidden ambushers. He managed to kill two of Knight's men, Dick Stanton and Dave Milton, and severely injure another Stanton brother named Ike.

Warner and Wall were arrested and taken to the jail in Vernal, but soon a lynch mob formed in the street outside. Members of the Wild Bunch, including Butch Cassidy, assembled to protect the two from the mob. When they threatened to take Warner and Wall out of jail by force, Sheriff John Pope decided to transfer the prisoners to the jail in Ogden.

Cassidy followed Warner and Wall to Ogden, this time backed up by some seventy-five ruffians threatening, once again, to spring them from captivity. Warner convinced Cassidy that they could avoid violence if he could get a good lawyer. Ironically, in order to be able afford the lawyer Cassidy recommended, Cassidy himself robbed a bank in Montpelier, Idaho. The effort was in vain, however. On September 21, Warner was sentenced to five years in Utah State Prison.

When he was released, Warner purchased the farm previously belonging to Caleb and his wife, Sidsie. On his deathbed, in 1905, Caleb drew a map of the Sacred Mine's location. Even if she could locate the mine, however, Sidsie would need financial help with the development. She offered a limited partnership to a ranch owner named Sharp and a doctor named Dowd, who, along with Warner, searched unsuccessfully for the mine for many years.

Although no white man has been inside of the Sacred Mine since Caleb Rhoades, there is one person who claims to have seen Carre Shinob, the ancestral burial site of the Utes. Historian and author Kerry Ross Boren says he spent six hours alone in Carre Shinob during the early 1970s, after being led to the cave by a small group of Utes. His account is chronicled in *The Gold of Carre Shinob*, published in 1998.

Boren makes an even more interesting and controversial claim about Carre Shinob, though. He believes it is not only the final resting place of important tribe members, but that the cave also contains King Montezuma's lost treasure. Legend has it that after the Aztec king was defeated by the Spanish in 1520, he had a large amount of gold and treasure taken north, to keep it out of the hands of invaders. Most historians believe, if the story of Montezuma's treasure is true, the loot probably never made it north of Arizona. Yet Boren says he saw the giant gold disks engraved in a foreign language. He saw the skeletons in Spanish armor, the odd jewelry and artifacts from an ancient civilization. If the priceless artifacts, gold, and silver were not from the Aztecs, where did they come from? Could there be truth to Isaac Morley's claim that the

Caleb and Sidsie Rhoades
UTAH HISTORICAL SOCIETY

artifacts were relics made by the ancient Lamanites described in the Book of Mormon?

It is not inconceivable that Boren visited the ancient Ute burial site. But if he is right about Montezuma's treasure, it would put the Aztecs in Utah over one hundred years earlier than the first Spanish explorers arrived—a proposition that most experts have a hard time with. If Boren really did get access to this mine, why haven't other people found it? More important, why would the Indians trust a white man with a four-hundred-year-old secret?

As it turns out, there is a family connection: Isaac Morley was Boren's third great-great-great-grandfather. After Chief Walker had become close with Morley, he gave Morley some personal journals, which made their way down through the generations to Boren. They, along with the journals and maps of a Ute named Happy Jack, came into Boren's possession sometime in the late 1960s. Caleb

Rhoades and Happy Jack were good friends who went on numerous prospecting trips together.

Between the journals of Morley and Happy Jack, Boren found the missing pieces he was looking for: the lost route to Carre Shinob. But he still needed permission from the Utes to enter the reservation. Once the Utes realized Boren had accurate information about the mine's location, they decided to allow him to visit, under supervision, if only so the eager historian would not attempt the trip on his own. This way, they could make sure Boren didn't walk off with any artifacts or otherwise desecrate the site. They also wanted to get his blood oath that he would never reveal the location to any other person and that he would never return himself.

No one doubts there is gold in the Rocky Mountains. The stories of the prospectors and gunmen, bleary-eyed with gold fever, are almost as dazzling as the precious metal itself. The possibility of finding artifacts or information leading to a lost mine or buried treasure remains very real.

If you did discover a bonanza while hiking through the Ute Reservation, however, federal law prohibits you from removing any rock or mineral. The Sacred Mine, now commonly referred to as "the Lost Rhoades Mine" would be difficult to stumble across anyway. According to Boren it is located high above timberline among jagged peaks, its entrance well hidden by rocks. Over the years landslides and avalanches may have concealed it even more. Boren has honored his promise never to reveal the site.

Can Boren be telling the truth about his visit to Carre Shinob? Even if we accept his claim of being there, and the theory that Montezuma's treasure is housed within, there remain unanswered questions. Boren says Ute guides had instructed him to travel the last mile to the mine alone, because they were afraid of a legendary curse and refused to accompany him. If Carre Shinob is so well concealed, how did Boren navigate a mile of rough terrain and find the mine's entrance by himself?

When Boren says the Utes would rather "concede controlled access than to risk my attempting to go there on my own," does he think they would be concerned for his safety or concerned he might disturb or loot the site? Either way, it seems as though they would want to be with Boren during his visit. Even though the Utes believe that certain sites are indeed haunted by the spirits of dead American Indians and Spaniards, the idea of Boren's escorts being so superstitious as to not approach the mine seems like a piece of fiction created to add suspense to the tale.

Will Boren be the last white man to ever lay eyes on the gold of Carre Shinob? Will the location of the Lost Rhoades Mine remain a secret for the rest of time? Or will the Ute's oath of secrecy be broken generations from now? Whatever happens, Carre Shinob and the precious contents of the Sacred Mine will always belong to the Ute people and will remain one of the great legends of Utah.

CHAPTER 4

The Mormon Handcart Disaster of 1856

The face of Patience Loader's father was pale even in the flickering orange fire light. He was too weak to talk, but he managed to use his last few breaths to tell his wife and children that he loved them. All ten members of the Loader family knew the trip would be hard, but they didn't expect *this*. They had come all the way from England to the United States—too far for things to fall apart now.

While the others sobbed, Patience wiped her tears away. She would have to be strong. In a few short weeks the trip would become a struggle for survival, and her family needed a leader.

Patience would become a figure of mythical status among members of the Church of Jesus Christ of Latter-day Saints (LDS)—not for the hardships she endured, but for the way in which she endured them. She set an example of faith and determination that kept her alive, while helping to lift up and encourage the hundreds of others who suffered alongside her.

For the past month the LDS converts had pulled their belongings on wooden handcarts across the prairie, from Iowa City to the middle of Nebraska. They were halfway to Salt Lake City, but the real physical and mental challenge had barely begun. With each step westward, the Rocky Mountains loomed larger on the horizon. As they approached the formidable terrain, the days got shorter, the air got thinner, and the wind blew colder.

By 1844 the era of Joseph Smith, the Church's founding prophet, had come to an end. Just over a month after Smith's death, Brigham Young became president of the LDS Church. Smith's murder at the hands of an angry Illinois mob had been a crushing blow to the Mormons, but Young used the moment to display his prophetic voice through captivating sermons, which turned the terrible event into a motivating test of faith.

Young knew his people couldn't live under constant threat and persecution, as they had since their church's inception. God, he had told them, was calling Young to build a *kingdom*, something much greater than what they had in Nauvoo, Illinois, which amounted to not much more than a few log buildings in a mosquito-infested swamp.

Young knew the best place for his people, the only place, was isolation. The wild, unclaimed western frontier would offer them just that. There were American Indians occupying much of the territory Young had in mind, but surely they couldn't be any worse than what the Mormons had already dealt with. Indeed Young believed he could manage them more easily and do their heathen souls a favor by making Latter-day Saints out of them.

For the Latter-day Saints, all the signs indicated a prophecy was about to be fulfilled. It was written in the Book of Mormon that God would one day lead his people to a promised land, where they could build a "New Jerusalem." As in the Old Testament of the Bible, Mormons call this place "Zion," which was both a set

With a spring in their steps, these handcart pioneers begin their journey.
Utah Historical Society

of moral codes, or spiritual state, and a geographical location, yet to be revealed.

By the time the Loader family had begun their journey during the summer of 1856, Mormons had been emigrating to Salt Lake City for almost ten years, as part of the fastest-growing religion in the world. That year there were almost two thousand, mostly European LDS emigrants, making the trip. The Loaders had joined a party of 576 people led by Captain James Martin. It was the last to leave Iowa City in August, pulling 146 handcarts provided by the LDS Church.

Another group of five hundred, led by a missionary named James Willie, had left almost a week earlier, with 120 handcarts.

Beside these two large groups, a few companies had preceded them, as had two ox trains, which followed the Martin group by a few days.

Of the five companies, the Willie and Martin groups would share the greatest suffering. It was the almost-superhuman courage and faith of survivors like Patience Loader that would make them the most legendary of all of Utah's pioneers.

Just after leaving Florence, Nebraska, the Loaders encountered trouble. Patience's sister, Zilpha, had given birth to a child near Cutler Park. When the main group left the following morning, the Loaders couldn't keep up. Alone in dangerous country, the timing was bad, but at least the mother and child were in good health.

The morning after they found themselves deserted, while the Loader family made breakfast, a man came riding up on a horse. It was Joseph A. Young, a supervisor of the handcart emigration and a son of the prophet Brigham Young. Surely after speaking with the weary Loaders, he must have sensed that they could have used some assistance, but instead of doing what Mormons are known for—helping each other and their community—he simply said something to the effect of, "Maybe you should name the baby 'Handcart,'" and rode away.

The following day a kinder missionary, William Cluff, assisted the Loaders by towing their handcarts a good distance, in defiance of Captain Martin's orders. Although Martin had offered to let the two sick people ride in one of the few horse-pulled wagons, he, for some reason, had forbidden other members of the party to turn back and help the Loader family.

The Loaders continued on and eventually caught up with the main group. It would take them over a month to get through Nebraska, and the torturous slog through the sandy Platte River Valley would not leave them in good shape for the final leg of the journey.

Patience listened to the grumblings around camp. She knew they had gotten a late start, but they had no way of knowing how brutal an early winter in the Rocky Mountains could be.

If the Salt Lake Valley was their destiny, the Lord would watch over them on their journey; of this, they were sure. Another thought that kept them going was the fact that other Latter-day Saints had made the journey. God had seen them through. It was hard, but it was possible.

Of course most emigrants had ridden in wagons, which was far more comfortable and less physically demanding than pulling a handcart. Why, then, were the companies of 1856 assigned handcarts?

Eleven years earlier, Brigham Young led the first wagon train of pioneers into the Salt Lake Valley, upon which he gazed and famously proclaimed, "This is the place." A huge statue of Young currently sits in Heritage Park, towering above the spot where the prophet made the famous declaration. In reality the decision to settle in the valley was debated and discussed over a period of days, but the idea of Young's divine revelation has been a cornerstone of Mormon lore.

In 1856 the Church was hurting for cash, which it desperately needed to fund large projects and expand its presence throughout the world. As with other faiths, the Saints had always relied on the generosity of its flock to fill its coffers. Tithing, or giving 10 percent of one's income to the Church, is taken seriously among Mormons, and such generosity accounts for the Church's ability to finance the continual migration of LDS converts from Europe and elsewhere. Because many travel expenses were paid for by the LDS "Perpetual Emigration Fund," horse-drawn wagons were simply no longer in the budget, especially with several thousand foreign converts from the previous summer still waiting in Iowa City to be sent west.

Young had been looking for a cheaper, more efficient way to get converts across the prairie, and he suggested the use of handcarts. They were cheap and could be built almost anywhere. The carts were relatively lightweight and featured large wheels for minimal rolling resistance over uneven terrain. The wheels' position near the center of the cargo platform gave the operator maximum leverage for hauling heavy loads. They could be pulled by one or two people, and with a small load even a young girl could easily pull one. Young's handcart idea finally took hold, but the theoretical simplicity of this method came up against a logistical and mechanical reality that would prove fatal. First, there were not enough handcarts for all the Saints in Iowa City, so more had to be built, which caused a delay. Another problem was the limited availability of adequate materials. They were forced to use green wood, which warped and twisted as it dried out, making for increasingly poor performance as the Saints progressed westward. In addition, the lack of proper bearings made for shoddy wheels, whose hubs wore out quickly.

It was no help that many carts were loaded with hundreds of pounds, not the fifty or so that Young had estimated they would need. As one can imagine, after hundreds of miles of pulling such a cart, even the strongest person would run into problems, even if conditions were perfect. As we will see, one of the only things working in their favor would be their faith.

Franklin Richards, a missionary based out of Liverpool, England, had been charged with the formidable task of assembling thousands of converts and getting them on ships bound for America. Once in Boston, they took a train to Iowa City, where their handcart journey would begin.

Richards left England on July 26 and arrived in Florence on August 21, just in time to briefly join the Martin and Willie parties before riding on to Salt Lake City. Although he shared Young's optimism, Richards knew the handcart pioneers were getting a late start, which would almost certainly put them in danger once the cold weather set in.

Prior to moving on ahead of the Martin and Willie parties, Richards wished them the best and promised they could stock up on supplies and food in Laramie, Wyoming. He also promised to send help back from Salt Lake with warm clothing for their final leg of the journey. Then he sped off in a carriage, reaching the Salt Lake Valley on October 4, just two days after the Bunker handcart party of 320 people.

Both the Ellsworth and McArthur parties, of over two hundred each, had arrived on September 26, and several other companies made it before that, totaling about 1,900. Of the other groups, there had been less than thirty deaths since departing from Iowa City.

Concerned for the safety of the Martin and Willie parties, Richards notified top church officials, including Young, that something should be done to help them. The Church's semiannual conference happened to be going on when Young got the news, so he made an announcement to the people, which was quoted in the October 15, 1856, issue of the *Deseret News*. "I will tell you all that your faith, religion, and profession of religion, will never save one soul of you in the Celestial Kingdom of God, unless you carry out just such principles as I am now teaching you. Go and bring in those people now on the plains. . . . Otherwise, your faith will be in vain . . . and you will sink to Hell, unless you attend to the things we tell you."

A rescue team of two hundred wagons was assembled and sent east in the hopes of providing some relief, but for many it would be too late. The Willie and Martin groups had barely set foot in Wyoming as the first snows of autumn began to blow across their faces. The short supply of food had been an issue in Nebraska, and many of the weary emigrants suffered from scurvy and other maladies brought on by malnutrition.

After reaching Fort Laramie, the situation became even more dire when they discovered that supply outposts had almost no food left for them. The Willie party, which was now farther along than Martin's group, had received a letter from Richards stating that help was on the way. But how long would a rescue take? Both groups were starving, freezing, and still over six hundred miles from Salt Lake City.

The Martin group faced their most treacherous and tragic moment on October 19, when they crossed the North Platte, west of Casper. River crossings had always been a dangerous part of overland travel, but doing it in cold weather could be fatal. They picked a shallow spot to cross, but their mistake had been made weeks earlier, when many had discarded extra clothing and blankets as a way to save weight. Before they even started to ford the Platte, temperatures had dropped and the pioneers were lashed by high winds and freezing rain.

At Red Butte, before the river crossing, two ox trains under the leadership of Captains Hunt and Hodgett caught up with the Martin group and helped them across the river, but the toll was still great.

Patience Loader recalled the tragedy of the Platte River in a vividly detailed journal entry. She described witnessing one man attempting to wade through the icy water with his child on his back. The man lost his footing, both of them fell in, and they were swept away and never seen again. There was nothing Patience could do to help, for she barely made it across without the same happening to her.

A few days later Patience had what some might describe as a hallucination, possibly brought on by the trauma of the recent events, combined with malnutrition and hypothermia. She wrote in her journal about a strange man appearing and putting her at ease with some kind words. He told her that help was on the way and that they would come to a safe place in the near future. The man then turned and walked away, fading into the snowy landscape. Whatever Patience had seen that day, hallucination or not, it was another affirmation of her faith. She had been kept alive up until now, and no matter what happened, she could not give up on her belief that God would see her through.

By the time Young's rescue mission had caught up with the Willie company, they had been snowed in for two days on the

Sweetwater River subsisting off of a few crackers. They had suffered terribly, losing nine people. When the rescuers encountered the Martin party, the situation was far worse. In the nine days since their disastrous river crossing, fifty-six people had been lost.

For both groups the good news was that there was food and warm clothing down the trail at Devil's Gate. The bad news: They were still a month away from Salt Lake, and it was only getting colder. Their test of faith would continue. There would be more sacrifice.

On November 2, the Martin group and the others, now totaling around 1,200, reached Devil's Gate. They departed for Salt Lake the next day and were immediately confronted by a white-knuckle crossing of the Sweetwater. It required great courage, given the recent trauma of the Platte.

The weary converts were grateful for three young men sent from Salt Lake, who carried almost each and every one of the emigrants across in their arms, dodging rafts of slush and ice. Later Young declared that the act would ensure the helpers "everlasting salvation in the Celestial Kingdom of God, worlds without end."

For the next three weeks, the travelers encountered rescue wagons that supplied them with food and clothing and also provided them transport back to Salt Lake. Although the handcart had been an important part of their lives, no pioneer from 1856 shed tears of sadness when he or she abandoned his or her rickety cart and stepped into a wagon. They were especially thankful they were not pulling carts when they hit the Wasatch Mountains of Utah, for these final 36 miles of the 1,030-mile journey were the most rugged and steep of all.

The first members of the Willie party arrived in the Salt Lake Valley on November 9, and throughout the next month, wagonloads of battered, frozen Saints continued to trickle down through Emigration Canyon. A few people died after the ordeal; many had permanent injuries, including amputations due to frostbite.

In total, the emigrants of that year hauled 653 handcarts and 50 wagons. Of the original 1,891 people in the handcart companies, around 240 perished, and between 135 and 150 of those had come from the Martin group.

In the following three years, there would be only five more handcart companies to make the crossing, totaling about 1,100 Saints. There were only twelve deaths reported from those companies, none of which arrived in Salt Lake City later than September 24.

Saddened to hear of the high number of deaths, Young did not blame the idea of handcarts in general, but rather the poor planning and management by Richards and a few others. Young vowed to kick out of the church anyone who started a future emigration later than a certain date, but he defended the use of handcarts, saying that a handcart could be pulled across the plains faster than one could travel with loaded wagons.

To prove his point Young sent a group of seventy missionaries east the following April, pulling handcarts. They made it to Florence only forty-eight days later, averaging over twenty-two miles a day. Although it was somewhat of a publicity stunt, the trip also proved that handcarts could be an efficient way of traveling, as long as the weather is favorable.

Patience settled in the Utah Valley, south of Salt Lake City, and married John Rozsa, a US soldier stationed at Camp Floyd. When he was shipped off to Washington DC, during the Civil War, Patience went along as an army laundress. She also ran a boardinghouse and completed her memoir, which is considered to be one of the best accounts of the Willie and Martin handcart companies of 1856. After the war and John's death from tuberculosis, Patience returned to Utah, where she remarried and worked as a cook at a mining camp. She died in 1922.

Not only does the journal of Patience Loader illustrate the details of the journey and its hardships, but it reveals the depth of her personal faith, determination, and courage. The inner strength of Patience has made her an icon for LDS members. For the secular historian she is a true example of the power of the human mind and body.

Although her story is at times almost too sad to read, the outcome, for Patience, can be celebrated. After all, she made it to Salt Lake alive. It is the less-fortunate who met death along the rugged Mormon Trail for whom we feel the greatest sadness when we hear of the handcart pioneers of 1856.

CHAPTER 5

Tragedy at Mountain Meadows

On September 7, 1857, a group of around 120 California-bound emigrants were enjoying a beautiful morning in the lush Mountain Meadows Valley of southern Utah. Their journey had been difficult, and they were resting up for the dangerous push across the desert and over the rugged Sierra Nevada mountains.

The group, composed of over twenty families, had traveled from Arkansas as a forty-wagon train with some nine hundred head of cattle. They were led by Alexander Fancher, an enterprising cattleman determined to make his second fortune by introducing California cowboys to his specialized breed of longhorn bull. Another expedition leader, also a cattleman, John "Captain Jack" Baker, was put in charge of the massive group of animals and dubbed "herd boss."

As the sun slowly peaked over the hills, the scent of cornmeal and freshly cooked bacon floated through the crisp morning air. Men and women were busy with their camp chores—washing clothes, looking after livestock, and making repairs to equipment. Children played in the tall grass.

Suddenly the crack of a rifle shot snapped everyone to attention, just as one of the young girls fell to the ground. Seconds later the group was engaged by a barrage of gunfire coming from the rocky outcroppings of surrounding hills. The women and children ducked for cover as the men quickly moved the wagons into a circle. They were scared, but they knew what to do. They had practiced defensive maneuvers before leaving Arkansas, and they had been warned of violent American Indians and roving bandit gangs.

Early on in the attack, Baker and Fancher were both seriously wounded, along with twenty others, many fatally. The Arkansans fought valiantly for three more days, but they had no idea what they were up against or that their fate had been sealed before they had even entered Utah.

Brigham Young had been encouraged by the constant influx of converts to Salt Lake City from the eastern United States and Europe. But around 1856 he became aware of a disturbing trend among members of the Church of Jesus Christ of Latter-day Saints (LDS). There seemed to be an increasing number of "backsliders," or those who fell into the secular temptations of drinking coffee and booze, swearing, and skipping church and meetings.

Increasingly angered by declining spiritual enthusiasm among the first generation of pioneers, Young came up with a plan to restore faith in the hearts of his flock, while teaching them to hate and defend themselves from Gentiles, or non-Mormons. He wanted to see a fire burning for the Lord inside each citizen of Utah, even if he had to light it by the torches of vicious mobs.

The kind of spiritual reformation Young had in mind involved a concept from the New Testament known as "blood atonement." A passage from the Book of Hebrews states, "Almost all things are purified by blood, and without shedding of blood there is no

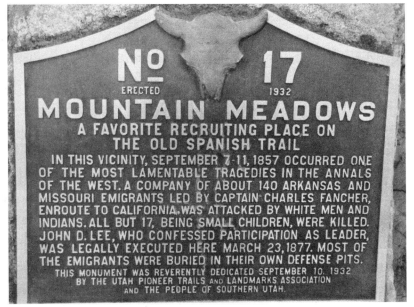

The memorial near the site of Mountain Meadows

remission." This idea was preached by LDS Church founder and prophet Joseph Smith and, back in Missouri, a band of vigilante Mormons known as the Danites carried out acts of blood atonement as revenge on troublesome Gentiles. One Danite, John D. Lee, became one of Young's most trusted men, in part because of his intense religious fervor. Lee would become a central figure in the Mountain Meadows story.

During the winter of 1856–57, Young, Lee, and Jedediah Grant, also called "the Sledgehammer of Brigham," embarked on a "Mormon Reformation." It was a frightening period in which roving groups of LDS officials presented individuals with a dozen or so questions concerning personal spirituality. They asked: "Have you committed adultery? Do you get drunk? Have you lied? Have you taken the name of the Lord in vain? Have you paid your tithing in all things?"

Unfavorable answers to these questions did not result in something so simple as a prayer for forgiveness. Scholars would later compare the reformation to the Salem witch hunts of 1692, which resulted in the executions of people, without trial, at the hands of angry mobs. In several cases LDS members who tried to flee the Salt Lake Valley were chased down and killed.

As news reports from Utah began to get the nation's attention, President James Buchanan felt it was time to put the Mormons in check and rein in Brigham Young. In May 1857, some 2,500 troops were sent from Fort Leavenworth to Salt Lake, but they were ordered not to attack citizens and to shoot only in self-defense. It would take nearly three months for the soldiers to arrive—plenty of time for Young to whip his militia into a frenzy.

On July 24, 1857, a Pioneer Day celebration at the top of Big Cottonwood Canyon drew more than 2,500 Mormons from around the Salt Lake Valley. Young gave a speech in which he firmly told his followers to ignore the federal designation of Utah as a territory and to henceforth refer to their new homeland as "Deseret." He also announced that all Gentiles traveling through Utah should be considered a threat and not be aided in any way.

Young then dispatched companies of the Mormon militia to guard the rugged canyon terrain east of Salt Lake. He also sent messengers all over the western United States to tell Mormons to return to the valley. He urged them to "Buy all the powder, lead, and caps you possibly can."

Finally, Young wanted to enlist the help of local Utes. "For they must learn that they have either got to help us or the United States will kill us both," he told Jacob Hamblin, who had been appointed president of southern Utah's Santa Clara Indian Mission. The American Indians, however, had been mistreated by the Mormons for the previous decade, and they were not motivated to defend the white man's "Promised Land" from other white men.

Three months earlier, on May 7, the entire town of Harrison, Arkansas, had come to watch the departure of the Fancher-Baker wagon train. And the procession was quite a spectacle—part circus and part rodeo—complete with cowboys, riflemen, cooks, a blacksmith, and women and children of every age.

Although covering twelve miles a day had been physically demanding, the trip was going well, mostly due to the detailed planning and organization by John "Captain Jack" Baker and brothers Alex and John Fancher. The men and their families had spent over a year meticulously preparing their supplies, and they had made several previous trips to California in search of a place to put down roots. They had decided on Visalia, just south of Fresno.

The Arkansans were not well received in Salt Lake City when they arrived in August. They found merchants and feed-store owners uncooperative and unwilling to assist them. Fancher and his men didn't understand why this new wave of hostility had come over the once-friendly and helpful Mormons.

The party had barely rested a day in Salt Lake City, when a Mormon elder named Charles Rich ordered Fancher and Baker to continue on their journey. He then politely suggested that they head south, where a river would lead them to a place called Mountain Meadows. There a spring could be found to supply them with water for the hot trip across the Mojave Desert.

Fancher had planned on taking the California Trail across the northern portion of Utah and on through Nevada—a route he had used before. Historians have always wondered why he chose to follow Rich's advice. Clearly his group was not welcome in Salt Lake, and Fancher probably didn't want to clash any further with local authority.

Before the Arkansans departed the Salt Lake Valley, Young repeated to his followers the order to deny aid to any passing group of Gentiles. Rumors about the Fancher party were reportedly spread by the Church hierarchy. The most famous was the claim that members of the Fancher party had put poison in the water upstream from a group of Pahvant Indians, who died as a result. Even after the Pahvants denied the incident ever happened, the myth was perpetuated for years.

George A. Smith, a high-ranking Mormon militia leader and a member of the Quorum of the Twelve Apostles, was sent, at Young's request, from town to town, warning people of an impending federal invasion. Of course the federal military forces had nothing to do with the Fancher party, but in the eyes of the Church, a Gentile was a Gentile, and Smith would not ask people to make a distinction between military and civilian Gentiles.

John D. Lee felt the same way as Smith, and when the two met in southern Utah, Lee told Smith, "I really believe that any train of emigrants that may come through here will be attacked and probably destroyed." Smith agreed, and Lee then told him,

"You must inform Governor Young that if he wants emigrants to pass, without being molested, he must send orders to that effect."

With a wink and a nod, Smith ordered Lee to "prepare the people for the bloody work." Much of the controversy about the massacre hinges on this exchange, because Lee was now sure he was under orders from Brigham Young. It can be

John D. Lee bore the brunt of accusations, but he may have been a scapegoat for other more prominent suspects.
UTAH HISTORICAL SOCIETY

argued, however, that Smith and Lee acted under assumptions rather than direct orders.

For the next month, as they traveled south along what is now Interstate 15, the Fancher party experienced a series of cold receptions. In one town after another, they were refused services and denied pasture for grazing.

Finally on September 4, they reached Mountain Meadows, a fertile paradise of succulent grasses and fresh springwater surrounded by hills. Here the party would be able to relax for a week or so and prepare for the rest of their trip.

As the days went by, Fancher felt more at ease with his decision to take a new route. The only Indians they had encountered turned out to be friendlier than the Mormons, who were all behind them now.

Each night during their trip, the party had arranged their wagons into circles, which was a common defensive practice for emigrants crossing unknown, hostile territories. When they camped at Mountain Meadows, however, their wagons were scattered about to provide individual families with some privacy. This break from their routine would be a fatal mistake, as would be the decision not to place armed lookouts nearby.

After the initial ambush, the group was terrorized by sporadic gunfire throughout the day. The frightened, wounded emigrants remained hunkered down in their makeshift defense fort that consisted of some wagons and a few hastily dug pits.

They figured they were under attack by Indians, even though Fancher had known the southern Paiutes to be a peaceful group. By Wednesday, September 9, they had been pinned down for two days, and water and food was running out. When two young girls were sent to the spring for water, some one hundred yards away, they were both shot dead by sniper fire.

Fancher, nursing his gunshot wound to the throat, realized that unless something heroic was done, the remainder of them would be doomed. That night he assigned William Aden and a man known only as "the Dutchman" to slip out under cover of darkness and search for help.

The two made it safely out of Mountain Meadows, and after traveling on horseback for a couple of hours, they spotted a campfire burning at Richards' Springs, near Cedar City. They found three men sitting there and immediately begged for their help.

Upon hearing the desperate story, one of the men, an LDS elder named William C. Stewart, pulled out a revolver and shot Aden dead. The Dutchman, who was still on his horse, managed to bolt from the scene, but not without being wounded. He made it back to Mountain Meadows and shocked the rest of the party with his story. The same thought ran through all of their heads: *If the Mormons won't help us out, who will?*

By Friday the situation was dire. A successful dash to the spring had been made, but there remained a shortage of food and ammunition. Decomposing bodies lay everywhere, and Fancher's wound had become infected.

Around noon a white man rode into camp. It was John D. Lee, offering his help. After identifying himself as a major in the Mormon militia, and a federal Indian agent, he told Fancher he could negotiate a resolution with their attackers. According to one witness, Lee told them that the Paiutes were responsible for the attack and that "nothing less than the surrender of their provisions, arms and cattle will pacify their wrath." Fancher and his men balked at this request, but after several hours Lee was successful in convincing the emigrants to give up their arms and possessions. He also assured them that there was a contingent of Mormon militia men waiting just over the hill to escort them to safety.

Fancher warned the others against going with Lee, but he was outnumbered by those who saw no other option. As one survivor put it, "It was either stick it out and fight till the last of us were killed or starved or take Lee up on his proposition, even tho it did seem fishy."

Lee broke up the 120 men, women, and children into respective groups. First, the wagons containing some of the younger children were lead out of Mountain Meadows, up over a nearby hill. The men were not in wagons but marched in two single-file lines, and next to each unarmed Arkansan was a rifle-toting militiaman.

The columns of men slowed down until the women and children were out of view. Then Lee, who led the columns of men, reportedly spun his horse around and shouted, "Halt! Do your duty to Israel!" The rifle of each armed Mormon was leveled at the man next to him. We may never know the extent to which they fought or tried to defend themselves, but the killing lasted less than a minute, and none of the men survived.

All of the women and children above the age of eight met the same fate as the men, while the younger children were spared and given to local families to be raised. Care was taken not to keep siblings together, lest they should divulge the truth of the barbaric event.

Later that evening, or possibly the next day, Lee brought the fifty or so Mormon gunmen together, many of whom had participated in the ambush and still had Indian war paint on their faces. He let it be known, through an intimidating speech, that none of them should ever speak about the brutality they had participated in. Finally, he told them, if the subject ever did come up, all of the blame was to go to the Paiutes. They "voted unanimously that any man who should divulge the secret . . . should suffer death."

Less than three months after the massacre, at Young's request, Lee drafted an official report that placed the blame squarely on the Indians. In his account Lee explains how the members of the

Fancher train had what was coming to them, because they had been disrespectful while traveling through Utah.

Oddly Young did not notify the federal commissioner of Indian Affairs of the attack until January 1858. Once he did, the Church had essentially put the whole messy issue behind them and focused their attention on the federal militia expected to reach Utah that spring. For his steadfast devotion to Young, Lee was rewarded with a twenty-two-year-old woman from England. She would be his seventeenth wife.

The following spring, as news of the tragedy began to reach relatives of the murder victims back in Arkansas, the story gained national attention, including that of Congress. Although Brigham Young had close friends in Washington who were already working the best they could to protect his image, the focus on the massacre made him nervous. He decided to provide Washington with a detailed "investigation" before they had a chance to get their own men on the job.

Young selected his loyal friend George Smith for the position of head investigator. What Smith came up with was similar to the account John Lee recorded: The Indians were to blame.

For a combination of reasons, the Smith report was enough to prevent federal authorities from asking any more questions, until 1874. There was no firm legal ground on which the government could try anybody for the crimes, because Utah operated under its own legal system and was not yet a state.

Young's helpful Washington connections constantly enhanced his image, and the subject of Mountain Meadows began to fade out of the national spotlight. Young and Lee had finally closed the first chapter of the Mountain Meadows Massacre, but it would be reopened some sixteen years later, when the Poland Act enabled the US attorney to take over jurisdiction of Utah. In September 1874, Deputy US Marshal William Stokes was assigned to bring down John D. Lee, along with eight others, on murder charges.

In the early morning hours of November 8, Lee shivered on a cot in a dirty chicken coop belonging to one of his wives, Caroline, in Panguitch. The day before, Deputy Stokes and his men had observed Caroline speaking to someone behind her house. Lee looked out at the sun rising behind the Sevier Plateau, and he noticed some movement in a thicket across the field. He jumped out of the cot and scrambled to bury himself in a pile of hay.

A few minutes later he heard footsteps. He lowered his head in the hay, tried not to breathe, and hoped the men wouldn't hear his pounding heart. Lee's eyes were open just enough to see the barrel of a revolver slide through a crack in the boards. According to one account, Stokes calmly warned the fugitive, "If one straw moves, I'll blow your head off." Lee gave up his own gun, raised his hands, and said, "Hold on boys, don't shoot, I'll come out."

Lee's first trial, in July 1875, garnered a huge amount of national attention. Many people expected Lee to turn against Young, but Lee had no intentions of doing so. The US attorney tried to get Lee to agree to a plea bargain and to give negative testimony against Young, but when Lee claimed that he was only acting under orders from William Dame, the offer was retracted. Maybe Young was untouchable after all.

George Smith and Brigham Young were supposed to take the stand on July 28, but they pulled the oldest trick in the book: They had their doctor write them a note saying they were too frail for all the commotion.

For his own testimony Lee claimed Young had not ordered the massacre, and his lawyers closed their argument by blaming the Indians. A modern-day discovery in the journal of Young's Indian interpreter details an account of Young trying to solicit the help of Paiute chiefs Tonche and Jackson in the ambush of the Fancher train. They refused to be a part of it.

The Paiutes claim that members of their tribe were near Mountain Meadows at the time of the attack, and they heard the gunshots and screams. The Paiutes steadfastly deny responsibility and regret that their testimonies, which could have been the most valuable of all, were ignored.

If the Mormons *did* do something so savage, Lee insisted, it would have been only because they were on high alert for Gentile military forces. This justification bears a close resemblance to an admission of guilt.

After a couple days of deliberation, the jury, consisting of nine Mormons and three non-Mormons, became deadlocked, and the case was dismissed. Lee remained in jail, and Marshal Stokes continued to tempt him with the promise of freedom if he would only point to Young as the grand architect of the massacre. But Lee's loyalty was stronger than ever.

Lee had always believed he was a true friend of Young's, but the shrewd prophet was about to show Lee that all of the trust built up over the years had finally reached a trade-in value. Young knew that unless someone was convicted in the Mountain Meadows case, his own involvement would always be in question. He decided to make a deal with Sumner Howard, the new US attorney, in which Young would provide evidence to convict Lee if Howard would leave Young and the other church officials alone.

Lee had no idea of Young's scheme, but he got a bad feeling when his church-appointed lawyers abandoned him. The standard "Indian defense" that Lee had used before was now crumbling under multiple testimonies, all placing Lee at the scene of the crime as a willing participant. Lee sobbed uncontrollably in the courtroom when these accusations came out. It was made clear to the all-Mormon jury that Lee ordered the killings on his own, without the knowledge of Brigham Young.

For his own alibi Young told a story in which a man named James Haslam rode from Cedar City to Salt Lake City and back, some five hundred miles, in one hundred hours. His mission was to tell Young that they had the Fancher party pinned down and to seek his advice. Haslam claimed Young told him to return to Mountain Meadows with orders to leave the emigrants unharmed. But by the time Haslam got back to Cedar City, the slaughter had already occurred. A letter bearing Young's order could not be used in court, as it has never been found.

For Lee, the verdict was guilty—murder in the first degree. He was a broken man, and although he felt contempt for Young, he remained steadfast in his conviction that what he did at Mountain Meadows was spiritually right and in accordance with the fundamentalist practice of blood atonement. In fact Lee's choice to be shot by a firing squad, instead of hanged, was probably inspired by the idea.

As he sat on the edge of an empty coffin at Mountain Meadows on March 23, 1877, some twenty years after the crime, he told

John D. Lee, sitting on a coffin to the left, awaits his fate at the hands of a firing squad.
UTAH HISTORICAL SOCIETY

the five gunmen to "center on my heart." Seconds later, shots rang out and Lee collapsed back into the coffin.

Over 150 years have passed, and the massacre continues to be a public-relations nightmare for Mormons. Family members of the Fancher party have always demanded an apology from the Church and were insulted by LDS President Gordon B. Hinckley's words at a Mountain Meadows ceremony in 1999. After dedicating a plaque in remembrance of the victims, Hinckley was quoted in the September 12 *Salt Lake Tribune* as saying, "That which we have done here must never be construed as an acknowledgment on the part of the church of any complicity in the occurrences of that fateful day."

At a 2007 ceremony on the 150th anniversary of the massacre, exactly eight years after Hinckley had denied any involvement of the Church, LDS Elder Henry B. Eyring spoke before a large audience, including family members of massacre victims. His comments appear in the September 12, 2007, *Salt Lake Tribune*: "What was done here long ago by members of our church represents a terrible and inexcusable departure from Christian teaching and conduct. We cannot change what happened, but we can remember and honor those who were killed here." It was better than Hinckley's cold disclaimer, but Eyring's words were as vague as they were heartfelt, and fell short of an apology. He certainly hadn't admitted any responsibility on behalf of the Church's highest officials, and many people remained disappointed.

The spotlight was turned on the massacre again when it became the subject of a 2007 Hollywood movie called *September Dawn*. Around this time the families of massacre victims voiced their desire for a true apology from the Church. Those concerned have arranged themselves into three separate organizations: the Mountain Meadows Monument Foundation (MMMF), the Mountain Meadows Association, and the Mountain Meadows Massacre Descendants. As a result of the pressure brought on by these groups, the Church has purchased an additional six hundred acres near and around Mountain Meadows, including the nearby Burgess upper grave site, in order to protect the area from encroaching development.

In 2011 Mountain Meadows was given National Historic Landmark status. Three years later, however, a California archaeologist found two mass graves located on adjacent land that had already come under private ownership. Since the discovery, MMMF President Phil Bolinger has been pushing to have the site awarded National Monument status, which would provide more protection from developers. "It's the highest order of federal protection out there and that has been our goal from the beginning," Bolinger said in a September 20, 2015, *USA Today* article. "We want to honor and respect those that were lost at Mountain Meadows in one of the worst tragedies in the westward expansion."

CHAPTER 6

Jean Baptiste, Grave Robber

Jean Baptiste was happy to have killed the free-ranging cow for food, knowing full well the Miller brothers would be less so upon their next visit to Fremont Island. By then, though—if his plan worked—he would be long gone, with a bellyful of prime rib. A week earlier he had designed his escape raft and pried a few of the sturdiest boards from the shack he'd called home for the last three months. It was a lifeless, desolate island in middle of Utah's Great Salt Lake to which Baptiste had been banished by Brigham Young himself.

The butchery was easy compared to the task of dispatching the grazing cow, a scenario that went sideways almost from the beginning. The way Baptiste figured, he'd approach the animal speaking in a gentle voice, get his arm around her neck, and then pull her close to his right hip, creating leverage against which the knife in his left hand could get some lethal penetration. He eyed a few big rocks nearby, not so hefty he couldn't heave toward the cow's skull if it came to that.

His first attempt resembled slapstick theater. Having gained the cow's trust with a soothing mantra, he was within reach when he tripped on a rock just an arm's length away, narrowly avoiding the heifer's skittering hooves while almost impaling himself on his own blade. The second attempt fell short of what would be considered humane, but at least he drew blood. He was getting somewhere. Unfortunately so was the cow, which now stood a hundred yards from the desired butchering location, blood dripping from a superficial nick delivered by the amateur matador.

The end finally came in a more savage and physically challenging sequence than Baptiste could have possibly bargained for. But it was worth it. The cow would provide much more than a few meals—it was the key to his escape from this godforsaken island.

Over the next few days he feasted on the finest cuts of beef, and sliced the cow's thick skin into lengths of strong cordage with which he could raft his salvaged boards together. Finally he had a finished product ready to test for buoyancy and maneuverability. The lake was so salty that nothing swam its waters but tiny brine shrimp that died off en masse, leaving a stinky, pinkish skein stretched along the shoreline. The fact that it's very difficult for anything to actually *sink* in the Great Salt Lake was of no comfort to Baptiste. He didn't know how to swim, and he wasn't about to learn in this lake.

Baptiste considered every variable in choosing his departure time and trajectory. If he went north to the nearest piece of land, he'd be less likely to encounter anyone, but he'd have to wait for a breeze out of the south, which only came every few days. If he went straight east he'd end up in downtown Ogden. Southeast, he'd hit Salt Lake City. Due west was the most uninhabited territory in all of the United States, and it was so for a reason. Baptiste was desperate, but he wasn't crazy.

There was no planned rendezvous or welcoming party. There would be no cadre of buddies waiting at the bar to hear his stories. After all, he'd been put on Fremont Island for his own protection as much as for punishment. Half the people in Utah wanted to spit on him, and the other half wanted him dead.

Some nights, sitting alone by his fire, a wistful feeling came over Baptiste, which invariably turned into burning regret. *I never should have left Australia*, he thought. But his mind never veered into remorse, the next logical emotion experienced by most prisoners. Feeling betrayed by the leaders of his own faith, even by his God, he boiled with anger. *After everything I did to spread the LDS faith, the sacrifices I made after converting, the long journey I put my family through. . . . It's not as if I killed a person.* And it was true: Baptiste had never laid a hand on a single living soul.

The evening he left, there was virtually no wind, and a dense, concealing fog had settled upon the surface of the lake. He tied his rations to the raft, including several pounds of cooked meat and a jug of water procured from the island's only freshwater spring. He rolled up his two blankets and placed them in the center. They'd get wet but maybe save his knees as he paddled.

He waded out with the raft almost a hundred yards before the salty water rose to his belt, and he climbed aboard. After a few frustrating minutes of spinning in place, he found a paddling technique that gave him some forward propulsion. Slowly, desperately, the tiny square of repurposed lumber inched farther from Fremont Island until it was enveloped by dusk, consumed by the mist, dissolved into mystery.

Most crimes are solved through diligent investigation, but it never hurts to have a little luck. The ghoulish deeds of Jean Baptiste may have remained buried in secrecy forever, were it not for the rash acts of a man he didn't even know.

Around January 15, 1862, Salt Lake City resident Moroni Clawson was killed by police after assaulting Utah Governor John W. Dawson. The federally appointed governor was not well-liked among Utahans to begin with, and when he was accused of making unwanted advances toward a married Salt Lake woman, word spread quickly. Sensing an imminent threat to his safety, Dawson attempted to board the next train out of town but was confronted at the station by an angry mob including Clawson, who beat the governor mercilessly. When local law enforcement caught up with the assailants several days later, a shootout left Clawson dead.

Officer Henry Heath of the Salt Lake City police was particularly sympathetic to Clawson, and when no family members showed up to claim the body, Heath pitched in for the burial, as well as the outfit the deceased wore to his final resting place. The Salt Lake City Cemetery would not be Clawson's last stop, however.

Some days after the funeral, Moroni's brother, George, arrived in Salt Lake to exhume the body for transport to the family plot in another town. Upon unearthing the corpse, George was shocked to discover his brother lying in disarray, completely nude. Outraged by such disrespectful treatment, George confronted Officer Heath, who was confused, having personally provided the deceased with sufficient attire for the afterlife. The odor of the Clawson cadaver wasn't the only thing that smelled funny to Heath, and he assured the irate family that he'd get to the bottom of the mystery.

Officer Heath went to the Salt Lake City Cemetery, where a multitude of witnesses remained predictably mum on the matter, and none of the workers seemed to be hiding anything. Someone suggested Heath interview an immigrant grave digger, Jean Baptiste, who happened to have the day off. Accompanied by a few deputies, Heath headed to Baptiste's home just a few blocks away, but the only person home was his wife. Puzzled by Heath's line of questioning, she wasn't very helpful, although she consented to a search, which turned up the first bits of damning evidence.

When he noticed several boxes stacked in a corner, Heath opened one to discover numerous articles of neatly folded children's clothing. Another box contained dozens of pairs of shoes. It became clear to Heath that any grave-digging skill Baptiste possessed was unmatched by his talent for un-digging them.

The fact that Moroni Clawson had been the most recent victim of an ongoing spree of posthumous clothing theft was shocking enough, but for Heath it was personally distressing, since his own daughter was interred in the same cemetery. Had her body been disturbed? The very thought had the lawman ready to assume the roles of judge, jury, and executioner.

Wanting to catch Baptiste off-guard or perhaps even in the act of robbing another grave, Heath paid him a visit during his next shift at the cemetery. Baptiste was busy digging a grave when Heath approached him.

"Know anything about any graves being robbed around here?" he asked. "There was a fellow buried less than two weeks ago, and when we dug him up he wasn't the way we left him in the ground."

"Nope," Baptiste answered. "I just dig the holes and fill 'em in with dirt. Seems like a lot of trouble to go through just for some fancy clothes."

"Who said anything about clothes?" Heath shot back. "All I said was a grave got robbed. That usually means jewelry. Can't imagine what kind of mad man would dig up a dead person and strip them naked."

A desperate look washed across Baptiste's face. He had dug his own grave, not with the shovel in his hand but with a slip of his tongue. At that point, according to Heath, as quoted by the *Deseret News*, "He fell upon his knees calling God to witness that he was innocent. The evidence was too strong and I choked the wretch into a confession when he begged for his life as a human being never pleaded before."

Heath proceeded to drag the groveling man over to a plot near his daughter's.

"Did you rob that grave?" he asked.

"Yes."

Then, pointing directly at his daughter's final resting place, Heath repeated the question, ready to strangle Baptiste on the spot should he answer in the affirmative.

"No, no, not that one. Not that one," he said, never realizing the response had saved his life.

Baptiste spent that night in jail and was brought back to the cemetery the following day to be questioned about additional graves he may have robbed. By then, however, the commotion had attracted a group of onlookers that grew into an angry mob as the morbid details spread through the crowd. Baptiste confessed to robbing about a dozen other graves before Heath and the other lawmen decided to return him to jail for his own safety. Baptiste made the short carriage ride lying under a blanket that concealed him from potential vigilantes.

To get a real idea of the anger and offense taken by locals—the families of the dead, in particular—one must understand the importance of certain clothing among Latter-day Saints (LDS).

Mormons wear a specific type of Church-issued linen underwear every day. The faithful are expected to be buried in these temple garments, in addition to traditionally formal white temple outer clothing. If a body is not in condition to be easily dressed, burial garments will be placed inside the casket, in preparation for resurrection when Christ returns to Earth. LDS families are spiritually "sealed," and expect to be reunified with their loved ones after death (or the rapture, whichever comes first). There are even documented accounts of Mormon families exhuming the bodies of loved ones because an important piece of clothing had accidentally not been interred with the corpse.

To Mormons, Baptiste had not simply committed a crime of theft and disrespect, he had violated dearly held religious customs in the worst possible way. How could they be sure, for example, that they would encounter their loved ones in the afterlife if they weren't properly dressed? This was a very real concern, and to put his followers at ease, Brigham Young addressed the issue:

> *It appears that a man named Jean Baptiste has practiced robbing the dead of their clothing in our grave yard during some five years past. . . . Many are anxious to know what effect it*

will have upon their dead who have been robbed. . . . [We]
have done our duty in this particular, and I for one am sat-
isfied . . . the saints will come forth with all the glory, beauty
and excellence of resurrected saints clothed as they were when
they were laid away. . . . Some may inquire whether it is nec-
essary to put fresh linen into the coffins of those who have been
robbed. . . . I will promise you that they will be well clothed in
the resurrection for the earth and the elements around it are
full of these things. . . . I would let my friends lay and sleep in
peace. I am aware of the excited state of the feelings of the com-
munity; I have little to say about the cause of it; the meanness
of the act is so far beneath my comprehension that I have not
ventured to think much about it.

On January 28, the day after Brigham Young penned his response to the gruesome turn of events, articles confiscated from the Baptiste home were displayed on a fifty-foot-long table at the county courthouse. Locals were invited to pass through to identify anything belonging to their deceased beloved. It was obvious, by the sheer number of garments recovered, that Baptiste had likely violated several hundred graves during his three and a half years of working at the cemetery.

The following day, at least a dozen graves were dug up and their occupants found stripped of their burial attire. Adding to the consternation of the bereaved was the fact that some of these pilfered graves were among those Baptiste had denied tampering with. They were dealing with not only a sick man of perverted tendencies but a liar as well.

Conspicuously absent from historical documentation is the possibility of a sexual element behind Baptiste's madness. When considering the context—both the time frame and the conservative nature of Mormon culture—it's not hard to imagine why necrophilia was never discussed, let alone written about.

Of course, we can't prove Baptiste was a necrophiliac, but the evidence points in that direction. Although it's been said that he profited from the sale of jewelry taken from the dead, obtaining such items wouldn't require the removal of burial garments. And if his intentions were to sell the stolen clothing, he made little effort to do so, but instead maintained an ever-growing wardrobe within his home. The clothes may have been a strange kind of trophy collection, yet even if he valued those articles above all else, one can reasonably assume Baptiste simply enjoyed spending time—which may have included carnal relations—with naked human corpses.

While in police custody in Salt Lake ity, Baptiste himself offered up a chilling backstory. He claimed to have robbed graves during his days as a gold miner in Australia. It was there he had discovered the Mormon faith and converted to the LDS Church. He said he had used the proceeds of the robberies to finance the construction of a small chapel. One thing we can infer from this voluntary disclosure is that it was made not to clear his own conscience, but rather as something Baptiste felt would reflect positively on his character. After all, he *did* build a structure that kept a few Australian missionaries out of the rain during Sunday services. It had to be worth *something* . . . As Baptiste would soon find out, Brigham Young didn't see things quite the same way:

To hang a man for such a deed would not begin to satisfy my feelings. What shall we do with him? Shoot him? No, that would do no good to anybody but himself. Would you imprison him during life? That would do nobody any good. . . . If it was left to me, I would make him a fugitive and a vagabond upon the earth. This would be my sentence, but probably the people will not want this done.

Baptiste sat in jail for three months while authorities deliberated his fate. Throngs of people would periodically gather outside to shame and threaten him, convincing the judge and sheriff that Baptiste would be in grave danger practically anywhere he was incarcerated. As crowds of angered locals grew, Brigham Young's offbeat suggestion began to sound better and better. But could it really work? Where could such a sentence be served?

Of the two barren land masses rising from the Great Salt Lake, only the smaller Fremont Island would lend itself to making Baptiste a "vagabond upon the earth." Although Antelope Island is larger and more inhabitable, the salty expanse between its rocky shores and the mainland was shallow enough even for the aquatically challenged Baptiste to make an easy escape. Originally called Miller Island, after two brothers who grazed their cattle there, Fremont was surrounded by deeper water, and it was chosen as the perfect open-air penitentiary.

To ensure identification in the event of his escape, Baptiste's forehead was tattooed with the words "Branded for Robbing the Dead," a bulky phrase that led to misreported accounts of an actual hot-iron branding. His ears were not sliced off, as some said, nor was he shackled to an iron ball and chain, a rumor that began when a rusty artifact of that nature was found by a duck hunter in a marsh near Brigham City.

In early May 1862, Baptiste was loaded onto a horse-drawn carriage and transported across the shallows to Antelope Island. From there he was rowed in a small boat about five miles north, to Fremont Island. He was left with a small shack for shelter and a few meager essentials.

Three weeks later, the Miller brothers came to check on Baptiste and reported that he appeared to be getting by alright. But on the next visit, there was no sign of the grave robber. The cattlemen did, however, discover a butchered heifer carcass, and hide scraps indicated the skin had been cut in a specific way, for a certain purpose. Cordage, perhaps. They also noticed Baptiste's shack had been partially dismantled. Could the missing lumber have been lashed together as a raft, perhaps with strips of rawhide?

Unverified reports of Baptiste's whereabouts began coming in shortly after news of his disappearance spread across the Salt Lake Valley. Most people agreed he had made his way north, toward Promontory Point, an uninhabited location from which he might have slipped farther north. Some said he was recognized in a Montana mining camp and that he even described his escape, using his real name. Other accounts had him in southern California, while many believed he boarded an Australian-bound vessel.

The story of Jean Baptiste is unique, not only because of the oddity of his crimes, but because of the manner in which his punishment was meted out. And, of course, there's the mystery of his fate. If he escaped but never made it to the mainland, why has the

Jean Baptiste is thought to have built a raft using cowhide and
salvaged wood to escape his island exile.
TONY FERO

raft never been found? If he got to shore safely, how could he have
eased back into society with that tattoo on his forehead? It's quite
a conversation-starter . . .

As with other stories of the vanished, tales of the supernatural
were spun by those who swore they'd seen a ghostly figure wander-
ing the shores of the Great Salt Lake. For most people, though,
the transgressions committed while Jean Baptiste was alive were
spookier than anything the grave robber's apparition could pull off!

CHAPTER 7

The Castle Gate Robbery and the Fate of Butch Cassidy

April 21, 1897, was a beautiful, clear day at the Castle Gate coal mine, near Price, Utah. The morning shift was over, and one by one charcoal-black faces emerged from the tunnel, eyes squinting into the noonday sunshine.

The tired men shuffled around outside the mine office, near the railroad tracks, hoping today would be payday. It had been almost two weeks since the last one, and the boss never told them when the money train would roll in. No one knew but him, because you just couldn't trust anyone in the Old West when it came to twenty-pound bags of gold and silver coins.

When Butch Cassidy woke up that same fine morning, he thought it would be a great day to rob a train. Now don't get the impression Cassidy was the impulsive type; he had spent more time planning this job than any other train robbery.

Sticking up the payroll train bound for Castle Gate wouldn't be as easy as riding alongside the engine waving a six-shooter at the conductor. Not only had the boss taken precautions by keeping payday a secret, but the mine is situated in a very narrow canyon, with barely enough room for the train, let alone an easy escape route.

As if stealing the wages of hundreds of surly miners didn't seem like a dangerous enough proposal, Cassidy planned on doing it right before their eyes. The key to his strategy was a well-planned escape rather than muscle or man power. Cassidy seldom fired a shot during holdups, and to do so at Castle Gate would ensure a most disastrous failure.

The fewer strange faces in the crowd, the better, so it was only him and Elzy Lay who slowly filtered in among the miners as the whistling train pulled in. The two notorious gangsters didn't seem to arouse much suspicion, even though their clean clothes and fine horses must have looked a bit out of place. Some of the miners had seen Cassidy and Lay riding on the steep hillsides over the previous few days, and they assumed the horsemen were training thorough-breds.

As Cassidy and Lay drifted closer to the tracks, they kept an eye on three employees of the Pleasant Valley Coal Company who were unloading cargo. Cassidy's heart pounded, but there was ice water coursing through his veins. He still wasn't sure the loot was on board, and he had to keep his cool. Besides, he wasn't the panicky type.

Cassidy knew he picked the right day when he saw paymaster E. L. Carpenter struggling with two very heavy sacks. It no longer mattered to Cassidy how strange it must have looked for a cowboy, or horse racing jockey, or whatever he was, to be approaching Carpenter, getting up close to him as if about to tell him a secret. Carpenter would have been confused as well, had he not felt the barrel of Cassidy's Colt .45 poking him in the ribs.

With a few quiet words, Cassidy got Carpenter to drop his bags. But the second man resisted and was quickly convinced when

Lay gave him a pistol-whipping. The third man dropped a bag of silver and dove for cover through the doorway of the camp store.

It was hard for Carpenter to comprehend the reality of the heist. It happened so fast, yet it seemed like slow motion, and he didn't even think of shouting for help at first. *Who would be crazy enough to do this?* he thought, as he stood there in a daze, watching Cassidy casually hand two sacks of gold to Lay, who had already mounted his bareback mare.

Cassidy's getaway did not go as smoothly. Babe, his trusty horse, was spooked when Cassidy tried to mount her, and she bolted a hundred yards, leaving the bandit stranded with a sack of gold in his hand. Quickly Lay managed to chase down and secure the skittish beast, which Cassidy swiftly mounted in a single jump.

By now Carpenter had come to his senses and yelled out, "Robbers! Robbers!" while someone else fired a rifle, but it was too late. Cassidy and Lay were off, up the canyon in a cloud of dust. Carpenter scrambled into the office to send out an alert, but Cassidy had cut the telegraph lines. The closest lawman was ten miles away in Price, so Carpenter told the train engineer to get him there as fast as he could.

The train, still full of steam from just arriving, took off toward Price the same way the bandits had gone. Carpenter had no way of knowing they had already passed Cassidy and Lay, who had hidden behind a small building only a short distance from the mine. There they outfitted their mounts with saddles and divided the loot— over $7,000 in silver, gold, and cash—among several canvas bags.

Once Carpenter arrived in Price, he tried to send out alerts to all neighboring towns, but again, Cassidy was one step ahead of

The Wild Bunch, with Butch Cassidy seated at right
© Getty Images

him. Joe Walker, another member of the Wild Bunch, had cut the telegraph wires in Price, further hobbling any chase effort. It took Price's Sheriff Donant several hours to get a posse together for the pursuit, and they wasted even more time by taking off in the wrong direction, back up toward Castle Gate.

Meanwhile Cassidy and Lay had already dashed south of Price and made an effort to confuse the posse by going in a large circle. There is disagreement among historians as to whether Cassidy divided the loot among more horsemen, in order to make the trail more confusing, or if Cassidy, Lay, and Walker rode straight to the Robber's Roost hideout, sixty miles south of Price. For now we'll leave hairsplitting to the academics.

Cassidy and the others were able to get away because they relied on the element of surprise. Of course it didn't hurt that they had some fast horses, which they were able to change every ten or twenty miles. Cassidy was on friendly terms with many people in out-of-the-way places who were willing to help him with his horse relay. He was well liked and people respected him, partly because he had not caused much trouble in his home state of Utah.

When the town of Huntington assembled a chase group, the man who took the lead was the very man who loaned his horse, Babe, to Cassidy. That posse never put in much of an effort. The trail found by the other three posses simply disappeared when it led them to the bright red rock of the canyon country. The hard surface held no trace of a horse hoof, and the landscape turned into a treacherous and confusing geological maze, impossible to safely navigate. The remote and difficult terrain made Robber's Roost an ideal hideout for members of the Wild Bunch and other outlaws.

Another favorite hideout was the Hole in the Wall, in Wyoming, located above a bend in Buffalo Creek behind a V notched in a wall of red rock. The spot offered a long-distance, 360-degree vantage from the top, and the canyon was a natural funnel through which any "rustler" could easily herd a few head of stolen cattle.

Cassidy didn't spend much time at Robber's Roost before heading north to the Hole in the Wall. When he got there, he discovered that the illegal cattle rustling done in the area had drawn the attention of ranchers and lawmen. It was too risky to stay, so Cassidy made his way to a remote ranch house near Buffalo, Wyoming. The home belonged to the family of Dan Hilman, who was interviewed for the *Deseret News* in 1972 at the age of eighty-eight.

He told a story about a man calling himself Robert LeRoy Parker. Although Butch Cassidy had used a few different first names, Parker was his real last name.

A few days after the Castle Gate robbery, LeRoy Parker appeared at Hilman's ranch looking for a job. Hilman was leery about the transient, but Parker didn't seem too shady, and even exuded a certain charm and honesty.

The rancher took a chance, hired Parker, and eventually grew fond of the stranger for his hard work and loyalty. Cassidy lived as Parker with Hilman and his family during April and May of 1897 before disappearing one morning, leaving a note that read: "Sorry to be leaving you. The authorities are getting on to us. Best home I've ever had. LeRoy Parker (Butch Cassidy)."

Eventually both the Hole in the Wall and Robber's Roost fell out of favor with the outlaws, as the remote areas of the West became crisscrossed with roads and access to such places became easier for everyone, including the authorities.

Try as he might to stay out of trouble, Cassidy became involved in an investigation later that summer when he purchased three fine horses from Billy Nutcher, a member of the Jack Bliss gang. Nutcher claimed he had traded cattle for them and that he had the title to prove it, but the money changed hands without Cassidy ever closely looking at the paperwork. The horses turned out to be stolen, and it was the last straw for the local ranchers, who had increasingly been the victims of livestock theft.

By the middle of September, landowners of the Big Horn Basin had formed a chase party to go after Cassidy and the horses.

Cassidy was used to keeping a low profile, however, and he never spent too many nights in one location. He remained one step ahead of the posse through the fall, and the chase was suspended with the onset of winter.

When April came, the leader of the angry ranchers, John Chapman, teamed up with Deputy Bob Calverly of the Evanston Police Department. They received word that Cassidy was hiding at a ranch near Auburn, along with another outlaw named Al Hainer.

Once at the location, Calverly was able to apprehend Hainer without a fight. Cassidy, however, would not be taken so easily. Hainer had been outside the cabin, near a sawmill, while Cassidy napped on a cot inside. Awakened by the commotion, he never panicked. His guns were at his side.

Calverly pounded on the wooden door, shouting that he had a warrant, to which Cassidy responded, "Well, get to shooting!" Both men pulled out their guns as Calverly rushed into the cabin, holding the barrel of his revolver to Cassidy's stomach. Three shots missed before a fourth shot grazed Cassidy's forehead and dropped him to the ground.

Cassidy and Hainer were taken to the Fremont County Jail in Lander and charged with grand larceny. They remained there until July 30, when Cassidy finally managed to raise the $400 bond from two local businessmen. A trial was set for almost a year later, because key witnesses were not available.

Although Cassidy was found innocent in the first trial, the rancher John Chapman filed another grand larceny charge for the theft of the second horse. The following litigation was complicated, involving many witnesses and lasting almost another year, until the verdict was read on July 4, 1894. The jury found Cassidy guilty of horse stealing but found Hainer not guilty.

Cassidy was shocked by Hainer's being let off the hook and began to feel that Hainer had worked some kind of deal with the prosecutors, both to ease his own sentence and to further implicate Cassidy.

Less than a week later, Cassidy was sentenced to two years of hard labor at the Wyoming State Penitentiary. He never served out his entire sentence, though, and was pardoned in January 1896 by Governor W. A. Richards. It has never been made clear exactly how Cassidy got the pardon, but some believe that he negotiated his release in exchange for promising to never pull another job in Wyoming. Once again Cassidy's charm had gotten him out of a jam.

His early release demonstrated the kind of respect that existed in the Old West between certain outlaws and lawmen. Cassidy was generous, and because he only fired his gun as a last resort (or so they say), it became easy for popular culture to embrace and even mythologize him. His story even made it to the big screen in the 1969 film *Butch Cassidy and the Sundance Kid*, whose characters were played by Paul Newman and Robert Redford, respectively.

The movie did more than anything to secure Cassidy's status as one of America's favorite characters of the Old West. Perhaps, in reality, he was not the good-natured Robin Hood that Hollywood has made him out to be. Yet it is difficult to imagine him as just another ruthless bandit of the high plains. He was more than that, but in the end he was an outlaw.

The final scene of the movie depicts the most widely accepted version of what happened to Cassidy on his final day. Almost eight years after putting the slip on US authorities, Cassidy and Sundance are killed in a shootout in the remote Bolivian town of San Vicente.

Many historians believe the two outlaws and Sundance's girlfriend, Etta Place, purchased a large ranch in Argentina, where they lived honestly for several years. US authorities figured out their location by illegally opening mail that Cassidy and Sundance had sent to family. Eventually they found out that a US deputy had been sent to Buenos Aires to find them, so they sold the ranch and went on the run.

With some health problems, and quite possibly fed up with the stress of being a fugitive, Etta returned to the states in 1906. Cassidy and Sundance returned to what they knew best. The following crime spree involved robbing several banks in Argentina and Bolivia. Beautifully executed, each job went according to Cassidy's meticulous plans. But the two men had not been so successful by being stupid, and they knew when to stop pushing their luck. During the following year, Cassidy and Sundance played it straight, working at a tin mine in Tres Cruces, Bolivia, until once again, they grew bored of their law-abiding lifestyle.

The two are said to have done a couple of large robberies before hiding out high in the Andes. What followed remains under dispute, for some believe the characters involved were not Cassidy and Sundance. A mule-train carrying a large mining payroll was robbed by two white men fitting their descriptions. Although the gunmen escaped with no problem, they made the mistake of asking a San Vicente police officer if he could point out a hotel for them.

The cop kindly obliged but was suspicious and sent for a nearby military detachment.

Later that afternoon Cassidy and Sundance were drinking in a cantina as they watched the armed men come down the street and take up positions, their rifles tipped with shiny bayonets. The empty town square was eerily quiet. The two old pals had come to the end of the line, and they knew it. They may have been outgunned, but they weren't going to be taken alive. With a few wisecracks and one last sip of beer, the two bolted from the cantina straight into a storm of flying bullets. They didn't make it far.

But was Bolivia really the last stand for Cassidy and Sundance? US authorities heard the story of the shootout, but having no chance to identify the bodies, and well aware of the duo's uncanny penchant for disappearing acts, they kept the case open.

Recently, historians Dan Buck and Anne Meadows attempted to use DNA testing to end the mystery of Cassidy and Sundance. The researchers traveled to the remote Bolivian village and had the bodies exhumed. Upon inspection of one corpse, bullet fragments were found, as was a leg injury similar to one Cassidy was known to have had.

After shipping some bones back to the United States for DNA testing, however, the researchers were surprised to find that there was no match between the exhumed bodies and the DNA of Cassidy's and Sundance's living relatives. Meadows and Buck were convinced they had dug up the wrong bodies, but no additional attempts have been made to find the right ones.

A bit less exciting, but far more mysterious, is the claim that Cassidy returned to the United States and lived for over twenty years in Spokane, Washington, under the name William T. Phillips. Several family members and old friends claim to have seen Cassidy on different occasions, beginning around 1925. Such witnesses say Cassidy spoke of traveling to Europe and Alaska after fleeing South America. He also told them that a friend in Bolivia, Percy Seibert, had identified the bodies in the shootout as Cassidy and Sundance in order to help them get away.

In 1934, three years before his death, Phillips wrote a manuscript titled *The Bandit Invincible: The Story of Butch Cassidy*. Indeed, if Phillips was not Butch Cassidy, he must have been a great storyteller, as well as a collector, for in his possession were several pistols bearing Cassidy's personal "E Box E" brand.

In 1972, contrary to the wishes of the Parker family, Butch Cassidy's sister, Lula, published her own book about the outlaw, proud to spill the beans about her long-dead brother. Instead of revealing secrets, however, *Butch Cassidy, My Brother* merely holds the door of mystery open and creates new questions. The book contains enough untold facts to arouse anyone's curiosity but enough inconsistencies to lead a skeptic right back to where he started.

Despite her untidy claim about her brother, the idea that Phillips was Butch Cassidy remains believable when we look deeper into Phillips's background. Researchers have never been able to find proof of a William Phillips being born in the small Michigan town he claimed he was from. And people he claimed to have grown up around say they never heard of William Phillips.

Perhaps there was a perfectly good explanation why Phillips knew so much about the outlaw, Butch Cassidy. Perhaps when Phillips died of cancer, on July 20, 1937, they really buried two men.

CHAPTER 8

The Great Utah Manhunt of 1913

Rafael Lopez bid farewell to his drinking buddies, stepped out of the smoke-filled saloon, and strolled among the ramshackle buildings of the Highland Boy mine. It was November 21, 1913, and winter already had a frosty grip on the Utah mountains. Any warmth provided by a few shots of whiskey was stripped away by the chilly air, and Lopez looked forward to retiring to his warm bed.

As two fellow Mexicans passed on the icy road, one of them mumbled something to Lopez under his breath. Maybe it was the whiskey in Lopez's head that distorted an innocent salutation, or maybe the comment was meant to offend. Some say Lopez had a grudge with the man over a girl. What we know is that he responded with a few surly comments of his own, reaching for his pistol, as one of the other men brandished a knife. A few seconds later, the knife-wielding Mexican, Juan Valdez, lay dying in a snowbank, while the other man, Thomas Carrillo, wandered around, dazed by a pistol-whipping from Lopez.

By the time Deputy Sheriff Julius Sorenson arrived on the scene, Valdez was dead and Carrillo had regained his wits sufficiently enough to pin the shooting on Lopez. Before long, a posse was assembled to chase down the volatile Mexican, but Lopez had the jump on them.

After racing back to his upstairs room at the McKensie Boardinghouse, Lopez grabbed his thirty-caliber army rifle and as many shells as he could carry in his coat pockets and took off into the snowy darkness. He was well prepared to fight but ill prepared for his own survival in the freezing mountains.

When he had found work in the Bingham Canyon district in the fall of 1912, Lopez wasn't the only miner with a shady background, but he was destined to become the most famous. The area had become a cultural melting pot, attracting the labor of more than twenty-seven different ethnic groups. The language barriers, however, did not prevent them from agreeing that conditions were poor—and the pay worse. The miners went on strike, and their bosses responded by bringing in low-wage workers from Mexico.

Rafael Lopez, one of the strikebreakers, was a hard worker who garnered the respect of his superiors. Aside from a fistfight or two, Lopez had stayed out of trouble. Not many people knew of his background as an outlaw, wanted for nearly a dozen murders allegedly committed in other states, but not many cared. Most of his coworkers knew him as someone who spoke English well, dressed well, had a way with the ladies, and could drive tacks at a hundred yards with his rifle. Some had even said he spent one summer displaying his shooting skills in Buffalo Bill's Wild West Show.

Lopez worked the Highland Boy Mine for a year, pulling long shifts in the underground maze of shafts and tunnels, until that cold November night when he finally let his temper get the best of him.

Rafael hadn't been on the run long before his feet were numbed by the fresh snow, which got deeper as he gained elevation toward the junction of Butterfield and Rose Canyons. He had left his good boots, gloves, and warm clothes back in his room, and started to wonder if they weren't more important than his bullets.

Within a couple hours of Valdez's murder, Sorenson had summoned Bingham Sheriff Witbeck, and the two men picked up Lopez's trail in the hills above Highland Boy. By nine the next morning, Police Chief Billy Grant and Deputy Nephi Jensen had joined in the chase.

By evening Lopez had made it to within nine miles of Lehi when he spotted a ranch house belonging to Edward Jones and his wife, Rose, who was home alone with her baby girl. Lopez knew he had to keep moving, but the wisp of wood smoke drifting from the chimney was a welcome sight, and the scent of fresh biscuits was irresistible to the hungry outlaw. He cautiously approached the ranch.

Through the kitchen window, Rose Jones saw the stranger coming and met him on the porch. After Lopez politely introduced himself and told her he was traveling through to Eureka, Rose offered him some food and coffee. He accepted and, trying not to betray any sign of nervousness, positioned himself at the kitchen table so he had a clear view out the window. As he ravenously scarfed down his food, Lopez did his best to engage Rose in small talk, while keeping one eye on the horizon. Snow had begun to fall, but Lopez had little hope it would do enough to cover his tracks.

As he sipped his second cup of coffee and listened to Rose saying something about the new house she and her husband were building, Lopez saw, through the falling snow, the figures of four men on horseback charging straight toward the ranch house. He shot up from his chair, pardoned the kind lady for interrupting her story, thanked her for her fine hospitality, and bolted out the front door.

The lawmen were still a quarter mile away, but the country was wide open. Lopez sought the only cover available—a small greasewood thicket. After scrambling into the brush, he crawled along a dry irrigation ditch, concealed himself in some sagebrush, and waited for the horsemen.

Lopez watched the men stop near the house and talk a moment before two split off for the ranch while the other two headed toward the thicket. Hunkered down, shivering in the snow, Lopez leveled his rifle. As his heart pounded through his chest, he pulled his jacket over his mouth so the plume of his breath would not give him away.

When the lawmen closed the distance to one hundred yards, Lopez took careful aim and squeezed the trigger. Billy Grant was dead before he hit the ground, and his horse reared up wildly, bolting from the scene without its rider. Nephi Jensen barely had time to figure out where the shot came from when Lopez fired a second round, which also found its mark.

When Witbeck and Sorenson heard the gunfire, they emerged from the ranch house, scanning the distant tree line for Lopez. A third shot rang out, and Witbeck went down. "I'm hit!" he screamed out to Sorenson, who dove for cover behind a woodpile, firing several shots in the direction of the greasewoods.

Sorenson wanted to stay and help his wounded partner, but Witbeck's dying wish was for Lopez to be caught. Jensen, who had been found alive, although in bad shape, managed to hold on while Rose telephoned for a doctor. It is doubtful any medical aid could have helped, however, and both Witbeck and Jensen died some twenty minutes before the doctor arrived.

What had begun as an all-to-common spat between miners, resulting in an unfortunate murder, had turned into a triple homicide of well-respected law enforcement officers. The community was outraged, and fellow cops were enraged. Thus began the most intense manhunt in Utah history—and Lopez wasn't yet done with his killing.

By midnight, armed posses from Lehi, Provo, Salt Lake City, and Bingham, totaling over fifty men, had converged at the Jones cabin under the leadership of Salt Lake County Sheriff Andrew Smith. It wasn't long before they picked up Lopez's tracks in the snow going south along the shore of Utah Lake. Sheriff Smith figured they would have no problem heading him off within a few hours.

Lopez was able to use his head start to rest and replenish himself at an abandoned cabin. The following morning he grabbed a couple of towels to protect his hands from the cold and departed on foot near the southern point of the Lake Mountains. Before long, he encountered a couple of sheepherders having breakfast. Still feeling confident about the lead he had on his pursuers, Lopez was happy to accept a cup of coffee and engage in a bit of conversation.

Lopez told the men, as he had told Rose Jones, that he was headed southwest, to Eureka. After the coffee had warmed him, he accepted a chunk of meat for the road, swapped one of the sheepherders for a warmer hat, and took off again. He headed south for a while, but just when he had gone around the point of the mountain, he made a sharp right turn, almost 180 degrees, and headed back north along the west side of the range. Lopez hoped the double backing would throw the chase group off his trail, but he knew it would be difficult with the fresh snow.

Around noon, as he crossed Soldier's Pass, what little energy his scant breakfast gave him had begun to fade. His feet were numb once again, his cheeks white with patches of frostbite. And no matter how often he transferred his heavy rifle from one hand to the other, the ice-cold metal caused them to go numb as well. Eventually he found a ledge among the steep walls of Long Canyon. The location was well hidden, providing a perfect vantage point for an ambush, as well as a place to rest.

Sorenson headed one of the two chase parties that finally caught up with Lopez later that afternoon. The lawmen couldn't pin him down among the rocks, but they knew they were close. As the group of about thirty-five milled around at the bottom of the canyon, the sudden crack of Lopez's thirty-caliber sent them scrambling for cover among the rocks and cedars. A second shot went off, the report ringing out for several seconds after the lead slug splashed into the dirt. None of the posse returned fire, because they couldn't be sure of their target. Lopez's gun had let out barely a puff of light blue smoke, and the echo had confused them.

Then Lopez shouted out, asking if Sorenson was there. "He's here, alright," someone said, to which Lopez replied, "Send him up. I'd like to get a shot at him." The rude comment set off a deputy's rifle and the bullet shattered a rock several yards from Lopez, who quickly squeezed off shot of his own, missing the lawman by inches.

A small group of Sorenson's men who had taken a different route heard the firing and were able to approach Lopez from a different angle to within two hundred yards. Although he was caught off guard by their volley of gunfire, the shots did no harm, leaving only pockmarks in the rocks guarding his hideout. By nightfall the resilient Lopez had survived a barrage of some three hundred rounds, answered by only about twenty of his own.

The frozen, shivering fugitive wasn't the deadly marksman he had been the day before. After the exchange of gunfire, Lopez embraced his warm rifle, trying to hold onto every ounce of heat from the barrel. But as another lonely, frigid stretch of darkness enveloped him, the blue steel became as cold as the snow and the night.

There was no way out for Lopez, and the sheriffs knew it. If their guns didn't kill him, the dropping temperature surely would. They ordered the posse back to the warm hotel in town and left only four men charged with guarding Lopez through the night. The authorities figured the chase was over, but their assumption was a terrible mistake. The mercury dropped even further, and the guards couldn't take it anymore. They either figured Lopez would not survive the night or they didn't care, but they abandoned the gunman altogether and headed back to town.

It was the coldest Lopez had ever been, but it was not too cold for him to manage a smile as he watched the four guards ride away through a silver blanket of moonlit snow. He couldn't believe his fortune. *Thank God I didn't panic and try to make a run for it earlier!*

Lopez was as tired as he was cold, but he was afraid that if he fell asleep he might not wake up. He had to keep moving. Slowly and painfully he rose from the rocky ledge, scrambling with his numb fingers up a steep rock face to a ridge before stopping to evaluate his options and choose the best route. He knew he might not get a second chance at freedom, and with his mind fogged by the early stages of hypothermia, it was hard to make the right decision. Yet surviving the cold night and putting the slip on the chase group had given him much-needed confidence, and he struck out on a brave and hazardous journey heading toward a series of steep shale faces.

At dawn the posse, even larger than the day before, made its way from the warm hotel to Lopez's abandoned hideout. After cautiously approaching the rock ledge, they were stunned to find only a scrap of uneaten meat and some empty pistol and rifle cartridges. They were able to pick up the track again, but it was difficult to follow through the steep terrain.

After a couple hours of slow tracking, the lawmen noticed that one of Lopez's footprints had become red with blood, and they knew the outlaw was having a rough time. He may have chosen the wrong kind of footwear for his escape, but the posse adopted a new respect for the tenacious Mexican. They knew it was not safe to assume a couple of battered and bloody feet would slow him down. If they ever did catch him, he'd be as dangerous as a cornered mountain lion; but even mountain lions don't carry pistols and a rifle.

As the noonday sun melted the snow, Lopez's footprints became harder to follow. The lawmen slowed down, but Lopez forged on. By that afternoon he had traversed east across the Lake Mountains and almost as far north as the Jones ranch where the chase had started.

By Monday, authorities had been chasing Lopez for four nights, and once they reached the high-traffic area of north Utah

Lake, they had lost his trail completely. Some thought he would try to cross the lake in a boat, while others figured he was hiding out in a barn or shack somewhere in the valley. All speculation was put to rest, however, when a few days later a man named Maurice Valdez discovered Lopez sleeping in his cabin, about ten miles southwest of Eureka, a considerable distance from the north end of Utah Lake.

Valdez recognized Lopez from a stampede and rodeo the previous July and was sympathetic to him, providing the outlaw a meal and bed for the night. Lopez slept a few hours before dashing out again into the predawn darkness. Over twenty-four hours later, lawmen got word of Valdez's encounter with Lopez, and soon a posse led by Andrew Smith, Henry East, and Sorenson converged at the Valdez ranch, where they picked up Lopez's trail heading southwest.

Authorities were afraid that if they didn't catch up with him soon, Lopez could find some friends among the Basque sheepherders in the west desert area and might gain access to a horse. Yet even with his thirty-six-hour head start, they were overly confident, Sheriff East going so far as to say they would have Lopez, dead or alive, by Thanksgiving Day.

Not far from the Valdez cabin, however, the track disappeared, as if Lopez had ascended into thin air. Sheriff East thought he had been tricked, and a cloud of suspicion was cast over Valdez. The leaders of the posse warned him that he'd better not be working with Lopez and trying to throw them off. With some investigation of Valdez, authorities later found out the two Mexicans had known each other, but none of it mattered when the real track of Lopez was discovered about five miles north of the Jones ranch heading northwest.

The fact that the resilient Lopez had circled the entire lake range to end up back at the Jones ranch was surprising enough, and no member of the posse would have guessed the faint track would lead them all the way back to Bingham and the Utah Apex Mine. That's exactly where it took them, but the track again became obscured when they got to the well-used, muddy roads of the mining town. They were close, but they'd have to wait for another tip.

While lawmen scoured the camps, interviewing people and searching for clues, Lopez was huddled in total darkness, deep underground, in an Apex mine shaft called the Minnie 2. He knew the Apex workings well and had spent much of his free time exploring the old, unused tunnels that led to other parts of the mine. Compared to where he had spent the last few nights, the Minnie 2 was paradise—a constant fifty-four degrees, with the cover of darkness, and the advantage of surprise.

Sometime in the late hours of the night, Lopez summoned the strength to leave his hideout and visit the home of a friend, an Italian named Mike Stefano. Awakened by the tapping of a revolver on his bedroom window, Stefano welcomed Lopez into his home for a cup of coffee and listened to the weary outlaw's tale of escape.

An hour later, taking care not to leave any tracks, Lopez returned to the Minnie 2 with a load of food, blankets, and Stefano's lever-action 30-30 carbine. The Winchester was a vast improvement over the heavy old army gun he'd been lugging around. After making his way a thousand feet back and down to a hidden stope inside the Minnie 2, Lopez sat in silence, trying to listen for the echo of an angry mob. He knew the reality of the situation. Yet even with the number of men after him, he was determined to survive, no matter whom he had to kill. For now, though, he could relax, and it wasn't long before the distant rumble of ore cars lulled him to sleep. The rest was much needed, and would not have been possible had he known his friend was about to betray him.

Having regretted his decision to help Lopez, Stefano told the mine foreman that he knew where the outlaw was. A few brave and vengeful souls wanted to rush the cornered fugitive, but they were outnumbered by cooler heads. The plan they devised was creative, but as we have seen, the posse of deputies was capable of serious blunders.

The next morning over 150 deputized locals showed up for what they thought would be an exciting way to spend some time away from their normal jobs. Sure it was dangerous, but lawmen had been killed and their deaths needed to be avenged.

Adrenaline ran high. Six entrances of the Apex Mine were manned by armed deputies, while oil-soaked bales of hay placed at the entrance of the Minnie 2 were set ablaze. Soon the shafts became choked with black smoke, and they stayed that way for the next two hours. The anxious posse waited outside in the cold, each hoping to get a crack at Lopez should the killer come scurrying out like a rat from its hole.

The hay finally stopped burning, the smoke cleared out, and there was still no sign of Lopez. A search crew descended thousands of feet into the Minnie 2, only to emerge ninety minutes later with nothing. They remained convinced he was still somewhere in the mine's vast network of passages, and when miners went to work the next day, there were numerous Lopez sightings.

After two Greek men reported a lengthy encounter with the fugitive, lawmen went to the spot, about 250 feet underground, with plans to set another fire. The task of getting the materials down to the location was difficult, and the commotion caught Lopez's attention as he lay in his dark corner. His hand slowly felt for the cool brass shell casings and his rifle and pistols. The stalk was on.

It's hard to say how long Lopez watched the men work before his Winchester barked out, flashing several times in the darkness. Two men fell to the ground, as the others scurried for hiding positions. The lawmen exchanged twenty or thirty shots with Lopez, but most of the lead found its way into rock or timbers. They still couldn't figure out exactly where Lopez was, and no one jumped forward to be the first down into the dark maze.

Authorities now had to deal with the problem of removing the bodies of Peter Vukovich and Joseph Melich, who were hastily abandoned after the gunfight. The following morning a group of seven or so, most of whom, like Sorenson, personally had it in for Lopez, were sent down.

Once the bodies were brought back to the surface, the lawmen moved on to the next phase of their plan, which was to seal the entire mine before infusing it with toxic gas. But it was another plan that didn't go exactly by the book. On December 1 another fire was lit, and this time a lethal concoction of poisonous chemicals burned seven hundred feet down, well below Lopez's hideout.

After entrances were closed off and every air vent on the mountain dynamited shut, the fumigation began. Noxious smoke seeped from air vents on the hillside all day and through the night before the blaze was rekindled with several thousand pounds of sulfur and black powder.

The tunnels continued to smolder for the next five days, putting 225 miners out of work, without any indication if Lopez was alive, dead, or had made another getaway. Some folks thought he may have simply walked out with a shift change one day. No one would question the boldness of Lopez, but such an act seemed unlikely.

When the burning finally ended, early on December 5, the barricades were removed and the tunnels allowed to air out. Later that day a search group spent four hours searching for the body of Lopez, but they came up with nothing. After finding only spent rifle and pistol cartridges, a storm of speculation intensified, as did the frustration and anger of the vengeful posse, which had grown to some two hundred men. How could Lopez have escaped, and where could he have gone? How could the lawmen have let him slip away, right out from under their noses, for the third or fourth time in a week?

Two days later, word came that William Kros, the same Greek man who had seen Lopez down in the mine before the first gunfight, had another frightening encounter with him. Kros was reluctant to talk about it, but the lawmen squeezed him until he finally said Lopez shook him down for his lunch, some candles, and tobacco. Then he threatened Kros to keep quiet, or else . . . and disappeared into the dark maze of tunnels.

Was Kros spinning a tale or telling the truth? Sheriff Smith believed Lopez was still in the mine, and was even more sure of it on the afternoon of December 12, when shift boss Sam Rogers emerged from the Andy tunnel. Rogers claimed to have had a long conversation with Lopez, who trusted Rogers as a friend.

Lopez looked bad and worn out, Rogers said. Yet the fugitive looked like a man at peace with his fate which, he admitted, was probably to die down there and remain forever in the damp, cold bowels of the earth. Or was Lopez just putting on an act for Rogers? What else might the outlaw have up his tattered, bloodied sleeve?

Lopez or no Lopez, business had to continue at the mine, and even if the fugitive was still alive inside, the sheriffs did not want to risk the safety of any more deputies. For the weary posse, many of whom were normal citizens with jobs and families to return to, the real excitement had gone out of the chase, which was officially suspended that night.

Throughout the following weeks, the all-out manhunt had slowed to a criminal investigation, punctuated by occasional sightings of Lopez. The leads were always chased down by Sorenson and others, but they always came up dry.

Sheriff Smith was eventually convinced that the Mexican had made a clean getaway from the Apex when an old miner named William Kingsbury showed him a route of escape from the Minnie 2 that used a series of long-abandoned tunnels.

Over the next seven years, there were enough letters written by Lopez and numerous eyewitness accounts to place him around the Mexican border, where it was likely he fought for Pancho Villa's Mexican revolutionaries. He worked his way into a band of outlaws

Apex Mine, Bingham Canyon, where Rafael Lopez was employed
UTAH HISTORICAL SOCIETY

and reportedly participated in some of the largest holdups of the time. For the next ninety years, it was never known exactly what became of Lopez.

Then along came Salt Lake County Deputy Randy Lish—a man with a passion for Western mysteries and police stories. In 1994 he became interested in the story after reading *The Search for Lopez* by Lynn Bailey. It wasn't until four years later, however, when he read *Manhunter: The Life and Times of Frank Hamer* by Gene Shelton that Lish felt compelled to further research the fate of Lopez. It was his own detective's instinct that got Lish wondering if the Rafael Lopez of Utah could, in fact, be the same Rafael "Red" Lopez killed by Texas Ranger Frank Hamer in a 1921 shootout, just north of the Rio Grande.

Lish had made the connection, but how could Lopez's true identity have been overlooked by both Texas and Utah law enforcement?

In 2002, after getting permission from his department to reopen the cold case, Lish traveled to Texas to interview Hamer's son, Frank Jr., who was eighty-four years old. Frank Jr. said that his father had known about Lopez and his Utah crime spree at the time he shot the outlaw to death. Hamer's Texas Ranger Company C was rewarded $3,000 for the job, yet for some reason the news of Lopez's death never reached Salt Lake City.

When Lish presented the Salt Lake County district attorney with the information he had obtained, they agreed he had solved the case. While there were no DNA tests conducted, the testimonies of Hamer and Frank Jr., both distinguished and trustworthy lawmen, were enough to convince the district attorney that Hamer had indeed killed the same Rafael Lopez responsible for six murders in Utah. The case was closed for good on January 24, 2003.

CHAPTER 9

The Faithful John Koyle and His Infamous "Relief Mine"

John Koyle was sound asleep in his Utah farmhouse when a gentle voice spoke to him from the foot of his bed. He sat up and rubbed his eyes, noticing a strange white glow in the room. Koyle's fear and confusion were quickly replaced by overwhelming calm, as he recognized the visitor, a bearded man in white, as the angel Moroni. The Mormon disciple could not help but feel honored to host, in his own home, the same angel that had appeared to Latter-day Saints (LDS) Church founder Joseph Smith, so many years earlier.

The holy messenger began to speak, describing a setting in the Tintic Mountains, familiar to Koyle. What Koyle saw in vivid detail, the angel assured him, was the exact location of a rich underground gold deposit.

Koyle couldn't forget about the encounter for days. It would have been easy for him to dismiss the incident as nothing more than a lucid dream, but there was a problem: Koyle had a history of premonitions and dreams that came true. By the time he was in his late twenties, he had developed a reputation as a visionary. Some considered him a prophet. So it was hard for him to simply let go of his dream about the gold mine.

John Koyle had many followers, but he never lived long enough to find the precious gold treasure he said the angel Moroni had told him about.

Three years earlier, in 1884, Koyle and his wife, Emily, had settled down on a farm just outside of Spanish Fork, where they made a decent living selling cheese, butter, and other goods in neighboring towns. Life was good for John, but since returning from his LDS mission, he had sensed a void in his spirituality. He searched for the presence of God in earthly miracles and hoped an epiphany or powerful experience would come along and make his faith stronger. He also wanted to understand God's plan for his life, but Koyle had yet to hear the Lord's calling.

Since the age of nine he felt like the Lord had been testing him. It was hard for Koyle to believe in God after seeing his own father crushed to death in a rock slide while the two were working a steep stone quarry. Koyle was tired of being tested. If he was going to follow the Lord, he wanted clear marching orders.

With the dream of the mine, Koyle wanted to believe he had found his calling, but he wasn't sure, so he decided to consult his LDS bishop. The bishop reminded Koyle that using such a unique gift of clairvoyance to obtain riches would be considered an act of the devil. Koyle explained that the money could go for a good cause, like helping the Mormon people, but he told the bishop he would do his best to put the idea out of his mind.

A short time later a man struck gold at the very spot in the Tintic Mountains that appeared in Koyle's dream. Koyle kicked himself for not staking a claim, but at least now he had more proof that he truly was capable of prophecy. Whatever his next vision involved, he was determined to follow it.

The Mormon faith, like other religions, began with and has been punctuated by spiritual visions, prophecies, and miracles. In the early 1800s, as a fourteen-year-old living in upstate New York, Joseph Smith had the first of a series of dreams and visions in which the angel Moroni appeared and commanded Smith to lead followers to a new brand of Christian faith. A specific set of instructions led Smith to a hilltop somewhere in the New York countryside, where he unearthed a set of gold plates engraved with unrecognizable text. It was only by viewing the script through two "seer stones," as instructed by Moroni, that he was able to decipher the foreign language. Smith's translation became the Book of Mormon.

The story revealed to Smith began with an ancient civilization called the Nephites, who roamed the Americas from 600 BC to AD 400. But like the Babylonians of the Old Testament, the Nephites became wicked sinners. Because of their inability to live righteously, God had them killed off by another group called the Lamanites, who Mormons believe were the ancestors of present-day American Indians.

One hot August night in Spanish Fork after a hard day on the farm, Koyle fell asleep almost before his head hit the pillow. At some point he was startled awake once again by the angel Moroni. This time Moroni told a story involving the ancient Nephites.

Before they were destroyed by the Lamanites, the Nephites had mined huge quantities of gold and silver from a rock formation beneath the hillside near Koyle's house in Salem, Utah. As Moroni described the setting, Koyle found himself traveling through the mine, which was more than just a vein of precious ore. One shaft led to a massive room filled with piles of refined jewelry and other priceless Nephite artifacts.

Moroni made it clear that Koyle had been chosen to find the mine's location, extract the treasure, and use the proceeds to help the LDS people. Koyle was instructed not to keep any of the treasure for himself, but instead he should start a massive emergency supply of food and equipment for when the earth is consumed by war and chaos, as predicted in the Book of Mormon. Koyle should name his project the "Relief Mine" and should use all the proceeds from it to sustain his people until they could, as promised by God, build themselves a "New Jerusalem." Although there were ancient Nephite passageways hidden beneath the surface, Moroni informed Koyle he would have to dig his own tunnels. He should name the five shafts, which he could clearly see in his dream, the "Five Fingers."

It would be costly, both in dollars and time, but Koyle was assured he would have the help of a "cream colored leader," or seam in the rock, which he could follow along deep into the bowels of the mountain. This leader "will mark your future course if you are obedient and work as directed," Moroni told him.

Koyle was then told he would encounter a hard "capstone" in the main tunnel, which would require over a month to drill through. Beyond the capstone would be a 175-foot column of white quartz, rich in pure leaf gold. The column would lead down to a massive set of nine caverns containing the priceless Nephite treasures.

The information made Koyle's head spin, but he managed to remember every vivid detail of the angel's descriptions. It helped that Moroni returned three nights in a row to ingrain the story into Koyle's mind.

Koyle was convinced what he had seen was real, but he remained hesitant to put his time and energy into something so risky; he asked the Lord for yet another sign. Finally Moroni returned again one night, telling Koyle that if his neighbor, who was digging a well, struck water at noon the following day, then Koyle should put his faith in his visions and pursue the treasure. The next day, as the clock struck noon, Koyle heard the neighbors shouting with joy as their well bubbled over with fresh water. Koyle had found his calling.

In early September 1908, Koyle and a man named Joseph Brockbank took a short hike up the mountain behind Koyle's house. Brockbank knew about Koyle's dream, and he didn't have much faith in the farmer's ability as a visionary. But Moroni had warned about a "doubting Thomas," so Koyle paid no mind to Brockbank's cynicism.

After hiking less than an hour, they came to a resting spot on the hillside where, ironically, it was Brockbank who spotted what looked like a glowing halo near the ground a few hundred yards away. They walked over to the spot, where Koyle confidently began digging in search of the cream-colored soil Moroni had spoken of. Only eighteen inches down, their shovels began turning up a very light-colored type of soil. They had *found it*.

Within a few weeks Koyle and some friends had staked out seven claims at the site. At first Koyle couldn't spare much time away from his farm duties. But when he found his chickens dead one morning and his children fell ill the next, he took it as a sign that God wanted him up on the mountain in search of the treasure.

He joined the five others, and they began digging around the clock in two-man shifts.

A growing team of believers continued to dig into the mountain, penetrating hundreds of feet, over the next fifteen years. In March 1909 the Koyle Mining Company was incorporated, with 114,000 one-dollar shares divided among Koyle and four others on the board of directors. There were 42,000 remaining shares of stock, which were eagerly purchased by LDS members who ignored the fact that no gold had yet been found. Miners also traded their labor for stock at a rate of three shares per day.

Although the Relief Mine centered around the Mormon faith, the LDS Church itself never endorsed or funded Koyle's project and was dismayed by the farmer's growing throng of followers. Koyle had recently been appointed bishop of his ward in Spanish Fork, and LDS officials wanted to make sure he adhered to LDS doctrine.

By 1914 the Church began to take formal steps to distance itself from Koyle and his questionable venture. Apostle James E. Talmage issued a warning to LDS followers not to support the false prophecy of John Koyle.

Talmage was a geologist, and one day after examining the mine workings, he determined it was very unlikely that gold could be found behind or beneath the type of rock Koyle was tunneling into. The pressure from the Church caused Koyle to shut down the mine for six years until 1920, when business was allowed to continue so that Koyle could cover some unpaid bills from the Church.

Despite all of his setbacks, Koyle moved forward with determination, and his hard work and faith seemed to pay off when platinum-bearing ore samples were recovered in 1929. Three years later Koyle announced his plans to build an on-site processing mill.

The idea for the mill was met by strong resistance from the board of directors, but the unflappable Koyle had become an entrepreneur. With the mining boom of the Southwest in full swing, it wasn't hard for Koyle to find investors eager to put their money almost anywhere in the Rocky Mountains. Within a short time the white "sentinel" building could be seen protruding from the northwest side of the mountain. But the structure was more symbolic than functional, because a working mill was never built inside of it.

One aspect of the mining business is that no one, no matter how experienced, really knows exactly what is under the ground. The very act of speculative prospecting is a gamble that attracts con artists and shady characters who fleece investment money from naive businessmen in faraway cities.

Skeptics may have thought Koyle was either crazy or a con man, but no one could tell him there was no gold, because no one could prove it. The State of Utah, however, tried their hardest by bringing in Dr. Pack, the most well-respected geologist in the region.

"In my judgment the Koyle Mining property offers no encouragement whatsoever for the future," Pack said in a scathing report, parts of which were printed in the January 20, 1933, edition of the *Deseret News*. "I do not recall ever having seen less encouraging conditions. The truth is, I did not find a single vein within the entire property."

Koyle had been warned by Moroni about the resistance he would face, but the faithful disciple had been reassured by additional angels in other visions over the years that everything from money to manpower would be provided for him.

Koyle's team had already blasted, chiseled, and drilled their way down 1,400 feet into the mountain. Nothing had turned up except a little platinum and trace amounts of gold. Nevertheless, Koyle's confidence was boosted when the angels told him he was close to finding the treasure. *It could be just behind the next few feet of rock*, Koyle thought.

Once again the warnings provided by the heavenly messengers began to materialize, as certain townspeople turned against Koyle, slandering him at every opportunity. They labeled him a charlatan and heretic. Yet the faith of Koyle and his followers was as resilient as the stone that dulled their pneumatic drill bits.

Koyle also claimed he was warned about the three deaths that occurred over the years. The first was a young man named Lee Gardner, who lost his life in 1912, shortly before he was to depart for his Church mission. Then, in 1934, an accident involving explosives took the life of Reid Weight. Even as he lay dying, Weight expressed his faith in the Relief Mine, stating that he gave his life "willingly and without regret." Another fervent believer, seventeen-year-old David Kunz, died under a collapsed earth embankment five years later.

While the Church officially condemned the project, LDS followers, including a few high-ranking members, continued to support Koyle financially, which kept the project going. Koyle's followers still believed in his gift as a seer and visionary.

The Relief Mine had become not only an expression of faith, but a community social event. Proponents argued that the mine kept young men out of trouble and gave them a sense of purpose. Many enjoyed the anticipation of the strike and were sold on the idea that Koyle would find the treasure at a moment of dire crisis, just in time to save his people from rapturous chaos.

Midvale resident Ogden Kraut worked in the Relief Mine for two years during the 1940s, and he went on to write a number of books about Koyle and the mine. In the May 16, 1999, edition of the *Salt Lake Tribune*, Kraut claimed Koyle was ". . . probably the only man I could ever say for sure was a prophet, seer and revelator. He was the most humble man I ever met. There was not a shadow of vanity or pride about him, but when you were with him, you knew he was led by the Lord. . . . There was a reverence that I have never seen, before or since. He was inspired. Anyone who met him could tell instantly. And someday soon, the church will believe it, too."

Although he was aware of the Church's reluctance to acknowledge his gift of prophecy, Koyle hoped they would be happy with his effort to prepare and provide for the LDS people during the hard times ahead. But he was made aware of the Church's true feelings for him when they removed him from his position as bishop, once in Spanish Fork and later from his appointment in Idaho.

As Apostle Talmage had done many years earlier, the Church issued another warning in 1945 to those among the LDS faith who were supporting or wished to support Koyle, the heretic. This time the warning was published in the December 2, 1945, edition of the *Deseret News* and signed by President Joseph F. Smith, Anthon H. Lund, and Charles W. Penrose:

When visions, dreams, tongues, prophecy, impressions or an extraordinary gift of inspiration conveys something out of harmony with the accepted revelations of the church . . . it is not of God, no matter how plausible it may appear. . . . It is our duty to warn against mining schemes which have no warrant for success. No person has the right to induce his fellow members of the Church to engage in speculations or take stock in ventures of any kind on the specious claim of divine revelation or vision or dream, especially when it is in opposition to the voice of recognized authority.

Koyle decided to make an effort to save any good standing with the Church and retracted his claims as a seer and prophet. Even after all the animosity toward him, he was still a part of the LDS family and had no desire to start a new LDS branch or sect. Koyle didn't see why there couldn't be room in one religion for more than one visionary. Nevertheless he issued the following statement in the January 8, 1947, edition of the *Deseret News*: "I do believe that the President of the LDS Church alone has the right to receive divine guidance for the people of this Church as a whole. . . . I hereby repudiate all statements which I have made against the advice of the First Presidency . . . and I hereby repudiate all spiritual claims I have made with respect to the mine."

A short time after issuing the statement, however, Koyle changed his mind again, retracting his signed statement. The reversal would cost him dearly. As much as he loved the Church, he could not deny the lucid reality of his dreams and the truth they contained. On April 18, 1948, the Church responded by excommunicating Koyle.

After his death just over a year later, the LDS establishment gave him a final cold shoulder, when Koyle's obituary in the *Deseret News* didn't even mention the subject of his life's work.

John Koyle himself may be just as big a mystery as the Relief Mine and the existence of the lost Nephite treasure. He remained true to his belief that he was blessed with the gift of clairvoyance, and some people to this day believe he was a prophet. Witnesses say that after claiming the Relief Mine, Koyle went on to predict not only the First World War, but the 1929 stock market crash, as well as the invention of the automobile and many other things that came to pass.

Aside from the mine project, we know Koyle was profoundly disappointed by his falling out with the Church. Were his final moments filled with happiness by the effort he put forth in God's name, or wrought with agony over having failed to find a single ounce of gold?

We may never know if Koyle was a true visionary, only that he failed to find what his visions told him to seek. Perhaps the Nephite treasure is still down there waiting, just beyond where the last Relief Mine worker laid down his tools and walked away.

CHAPTER 10

The Legend of the Josephine de Martinique

In 1939 John Young Jr., a fifty-year-old grandson of the Prophet Brigham Young, was living with his family on the Weber River, near Oakley, Utah. A successful cattleman, he frequently grazed his herd along the slopes of Hoyt Peak, just east of Kamas.

One day while tending the animals with his twelve-year-old son Keith, an afternoon thunderstorm made its way toward them. Lightning flashed, and rain began to fall. As the rain turned to hail, John and Keith scrambled for cover behind a stone ledge on the northeast side of the mountain. John pulled a canteen from his pack, took a long sip, and turned to hand the canteen to his son. But the boy was gone.

Where his son had been, there was now a hole in the ground. After a moment of panic, John was relieved to hear his son's voice echo, "I'm okaaay!"

It must have been a large cavern. John cautiously descended through the opening to investigate. The little bit of light from the entrance hole revealed a room about forty feet long and twenty feet wide. This was no natural cave but some kind of old mine workings. Not wanting to disturb anything, they scrambled up the slippery stones, wriggling through the small tear in the sod, and headed back to camp.

When they returned to the hole later with flashlights, they observed old tools scattered about—blacksmith tongs, chisels, hammers—as if the miners had taken a lunch break only hours ago. John explored a tunnel leading at an angle from the main room to a large wooden door. The dusty flashlight beam revealed a heavy chain around the door, secured by a large padlock. They climbed out, covered the entrance with rocks, and headed back down the mountain, stumbling with excitement.

John didn't like to get worked up about things, but he had heard too many tales of lost Spanish mines to stay calm. He didn't think for a minute he had found the famed Josephine, known as one of the richest gold and silver mines in North America. The Henry Mountain Range far to the south was the only place Young had ever heard the Josephine might be. No, Young thought they may have discovered one of the Lost Rhoades Mines, or one of many other Spanish workings, but as the two descended they knew they were onto *something*.

It is believed that Spaniards made their way north into the Utah area as early as the mid-seventeenth century. Gold and silver mining, however, did get going until many years later. We know that in 1718 Don Pedro Garcia, the governor of the Mexican province Isleta, was sent into the Uinta Mountains to explore for gold. In 1722 he claimed the area around Hoyt Peak, and the Garcia Mines were operated until 1745. One of Don Pedro's sons, Jose Garcia, reopened the mine in 1779, calling it Josephine de la Martinique, after the French empress born on the Caribbean island of Martinique six years earlier.

There is documented proof of the mine's existence in the form of Spanish and Mexican church records. Although the shipping documents mention the gold from the Josephine originating somewhere in the Utah territory, they do not indicate exactly where. Over the years people have claimed to discover the lost Josephine at several different Utah locations. Around 1897 prospector Frank Lawler found a tunnel about thirty feet underground near Crescent Creek, in the Henry Mountains of southern Utah. Believing he had found the Josephine, he tried to excavate further, but the tunnel filled with water and Lawler gave up.

A short time later Ed Wolverton discovered some Spanish mine workings in the same area, as well as old symbols carved into trees. For the next twenty years, Wolverton scoured the Henrys, trying to find some proof of the Josephine among the old workings. Two inscriptions found in nearby sandstone walls fueled speculation that the fabled treasure was located in the Henrys. One reads, "1642 Ano Dom" and the other "De Julio 1661."

Then in 1908 George Olson claimed he had found the Josephine on Currant Creek, outside of Heber, hundreds of miles north of the Henrys. Once again the presence of Spanish artifacts got everyone's attention, even if the presence of gold was yet to be proven. An article in the *Mining Review* piqued the interest of investors who wanted a piece of the action.

While Olson was confident of his discovery, the absence of gold ore worried him, so he and his business partners came up with a plan to make the project a little more promising to investors. The "salting" of claims had been done many times before, during mining booms of all kinds. Olson's men took pieces of high-grade ore and stuck it to the walls of the mine shaft. But just before they were to bring investors in to have a look, Olson had second thoughts about the scam and came clean. The entire event made for great headlines and campfire gossip and added to the mystery of the Josephine.

The account of John W. Young Jr., the next man to come across the Josephine, is the most exciting. Irony abounds on many levels, for Young did not believe his discovery was the Josephine, yet he would not live long enough to see the proof that it almost certainly *was* the Josephine.

When John and Keith Young returned to tell their family about their discovery on Hoyt Peak, John said they had found one of the lost Rhoades Mines. These were legendary Spanish mines from which the Latter-day Saints Church supposedly obtained huge amounts of gold when the Salt Lake Valley was settled. Still, John wasn't sure what he had found—and it didn't really matter, because after filing a claim on September 15, 1939, the aptly named "Mystery Mine" was all *his*.

John and his sons were eager to get back to the site for exploration, but winter came early that year. And when his oldest, Marion, was shipped off to war the following spring, the project was put on hold.

The main thing Young needed now was money to buy machinery for the excavation. Young could have solicited help from other people, but he wanted to keep his find a secret. For the next few years, he did some more exploration of Hoyt Peak, while waiting for the right opportunity to work on his Mystery Mine.

Young had shown discipline and prudence in his decision not to rush back into the mine. He knew that if he made any mistakes, the shaft could cave in and injure or kill someone and make the rest of the job of getting to any treasure much harder. Yet by the summer of 1944, Young's gold fever got the best of him and his approach shifted from conservative to reckless. He made a crude plan to try to dislodge the padlocked wooden door using blasting caps and black powder. After putting the explosives in place, he lit the fuse and scurried back toward the surface. Before he got out, though, his headlamp's beam swung across a small pile of gray bricks in the corner. He hadn't noticed them before, but there wasn't any time to have a closer look, so he snatched one of the pieces, put it in his pocket, and climbed out of the mine. Less than a minute later, a giant explosion shook the hillside. It was a much bigger detonation than Young had expected.

While waiting for the dust to clear, Young reached in his pocket for the brick he had taken. Nothing seemed special about the dull piece, until Young used a sharp rock to scratch the surface, revealing a bright metallic material. The bar was a chunk of pure silver! But Young's excitement quickly turned to somber sadness when the cloud of pulverized stone dissipated to reveal a disaster: The main room of the mine had caved in, obstructing all access to the wooden door and anything that lay beyond.

Young could not afford the excavation of the caved-in mine, and he didn't like the idea of searching for investors. He had heard stories of prospectors being swindled by "businessmen" who turned out to be nothing more than smooth-talking claim jumpers. The project was abandoned, and the Mystery Mine claim became invalid, as Young failed to pay the annual property tax.

For the next fifteen years, Young stewed in the memory of his blunder, until 1960, when a man named McBee introduced him to Tumejewel, a 103-year-old Ute. Old "Tommy" told an amazing tale of a Spaniard known as Black Whiskers, who had visited the area around 1870. The story picks up on a steep, overgrown path high in the Uinta Mountains. Black Whiskers and two other Spaniards traversed the rugged terrain with a small group of Mexicans—slave workers brought along from California. The prospectors had obtained a map to an old mine, called the Josephine, which had been worked by his ancestors nearly 150 years earlier. By the 1800s the Josephine already had a reputation as being one of the richest mines in the New World. The Spaniards were determined to find and reopen it.

When the weary group finally found the mine, Black Whiskers stopped, wiped the sweat from his brow, and puffed on a cigar as he examined the surrounding terrain. After a conference with his two men, he decided they should get more help for the huge project. They found such help in several local Utes, whom the Spaniards abducted and promptly put to work.

Over the course of a few months, the crew had extracted enough rich ore to produce a large number of pure gold bars, which were stacked neatly behind a heavy wooden door not far inside the entrance. Other Indians soon got word of the hostile Spaniards and decided to act. A small party of Ute warriors was assembled, and they brought along ten-year-old Tumejewel.

After hiking to the Josephine, the warriors took hiding places with their rifles and waited for the miners to come out. Several hours later a group of dust-covered Indians and Mexicans emerged, squinting in the afternoon sunlight. The patient Utes made sure they could clearly see who was in charge and fixed their sights on Black Whiskers and his two compatriots. A few shots rang out, and when the smoke cleared, the three Spaniards were dead and the enslaved Indians were free.

As for the Mexicans, they buried the dead men and were sternly told to leave and never return. But the Utes did not trust the Mexicans and dispatched a couple of stealthy spies to keep track of them. A few weeks later, just as the Utes had figured, the Mexicans came back and made off with as much gold and silver as their burros could haul. As they headed down the mountain, they were confronted by the Utes and forced to bury the sparkling booty on the spot. Feeling lucky to get away with their lives, the Mexicans never returned to the site.

John Young could barely believe his ears. *The wooden door! The padlock! Could it really be the same mine?* As he listened to Tommy, he felt himself coming down with a severe case of gold fever. And with it came the bitterness of his failures—and the reality of the task at hand.

He wished it would be as easy as it sounded, but there was more than just a pile of rocks between himself and that wooden door. He was getting old. He didn't have much energy, and he surely didn't have the finances. Perhaps this is the real reason Young still refused to believe his mine was actually the Josephine. To know it was, while not being able to get at it, would be to suffocate in a mire of regrets. Still, he had to try. As long as he was alive, he could search for buried treasure.

Without the funds to explore the Mystery Mine further, Young and McBee turned their attention to the gold bars buried by the Mexicans Tommy had spoken of. Such a treasure could lie just inches below the very ground they had walked a thousand times. The two decided to file several "placer" claims on a ridge near where they believed the gold might be.

Then, in the fall of 1962, opportunity knocked once more. This time it was the coal delivery man named Don Johnson at the front door of Young's house. After a long discussion that veered into lost Spanish mines, the two men realized they might be able to help each other. Johnson had the equipment required to excavate the caved-in Mystery Mine, and more important, he knew a man named Jack Olsen who had money to invest in risky ventures. As for Young, well, he had nothing to lose.

Olsen was interested in the project and brought forth a man in named Newell Carter, who convinced Young that they should acquire official maps for use in reclaiming the Mystery Mine. Young reluctantly went to the State Highway Department for the maps, where he met a few students who said they were looking for an old Spanish mine called the Josephine, around Hoyt Peak. Their own treasure map would eventually lead them to Young's mine, but not before Young and his partners reclaimed the Mystery Mine on October 30, 1962.

They also placed claims on two other nearby sites. The first was an outcropping of rich ore they called the Black Nugget vein, found by John while Marion was away at war. The other claim was a hole in the ground, not far from the Mystery Mine, which they named the Glory Hole. Johnson explored this hole and found several tunnels splitting off in different directions. It looked interesting, even promising, but it would have to wait.

The summer of 1963 was spent building the road up to the mine, with the help of a Caterpillar backhoe purchased for $10,000 by Young's new investors. The following spring the first order of business was the exploration of the Glory Hole. Young was disappointed to find that the event had become a circus. There were numerous townspeople on hand, cattlemen, a University of Utah professor, and the same three students Young had met at the Highway Department.

After getting a few reports of the shafts leading from the Glory Hole, Young and Carter proposed that they attempt to intersect the Mystery Mine from the backside. Johnson disagreed, however, arguing they should approach the Mystery Mine from a small space near the main room, which had not yet fully collapsed. The wooden door could still be seen through a few gaps in the rubble, and Johnson figured a few controlled blasts could clear the way.

Since Young was not funding the operation, his advice was not heeded and the blasting commenced. Johnson immediately realized his folly. The explosion caused an even more severe collapse of the main room and a complete obstruction of the tunnel and its wooden door. Young knew more about the mine than anyone, and "Plan B" was to start listening to him.

Not wanting to take direction from Young, the four business partners ended their relationship and moved their equipment off the mountain, while Young retained the rights to his claims. He may have been discouraged, but he wasn't defeated. Two good things had come from the ordeal—a cabin had been built near the site and a good access road was made. Young had been keeping up with his annual assessments, but when the Forest Service burned down his cabin, he began to lose hope once again.

Then in 1967, Young's cousin Lavar Shurtz offered to put forth his time and equipment to dig away the entrance. The two men filed new claims on Hoyt Peak and used a backhoe to dig a trench near the Black Nugget and Climax claims. The ore they extracted, rich in gold, silver, copper, iron, and titanium, was indeed of very high value—as much as $200,000 per ton.

While the news from the assayer's office excited Young and Shurtz, they were disappointed to learn that it would be difficult and expensive to isolate precious metals from this type of rock. In fact there were only a few refineries in the world capable of dealing with such complex ore. Once again Young was spinning his wheels. He could see the pot of gold, but he just couldn't get to the end of the rainbow.

At seventy-nine years old, Young's quest for gold was no longer just about adventure and the hope of success. Sure he wanted the payoff, but the real reward would be in knowing that he had not squandered his time, that all those years of digging and dreaming would somehow be validated.

Young died on June 8, 1981, without ever striking it rich on Hoyt Peak. But his efforts were not a failure. Had he paid more attention to the university students and their Spanish map, Young may have been convinced that the Mystery Mine really *was* the Josephine. Although the discovery would have been historically significant, it is hard to say just how Young would have changed his approach to the excavation.

Instead, the positive identification of the Josephine would have to wait some twenty years, when author and western mine expert Stephen Shaffer concluded his years of research. After studying journals and maps of the Garcia family, to whom the original Josephine claims belonged, Shaffer was able to find convincing evidence of the Josephine's true location, which he published in his 2005 book, *Out of the Dust*.

As it turned out, the Josephine was not a single mine shaft, but a group of seven mines, the largest of them presumably Young's Mystery Mine. Shaffer claims the Garcia map in his possession indicates a complex of mines near the Santa Ana River, now called the Weber. These maps were not the same maps carried by the college students, but they were drawn by Garcia himself, at the request of the Spanish government.

Interestingly, although he is free with sharing GPS coordinates of the Josephine and others sites, Shaffer did not include the Garcia maps in his book. He did, however, explain his reasoning via e-mail communication with the author of this book. "I didn't put the maps of the Garcia in [my] book because I am still using them to find other mines and sites," he said. "I doubt very much that I will ever be publishing them or let anyone see them. I had to pay dearly for them!"

Shaffer does not explain how he came into possession of the maps, but the information from Garcia's expedition journal is available to the public at the Mexican National Archives in Mexico City.

Can Shaffer really lay claim to being the first and only researcher to have solved a Spanish mine mystery? He has almost certainly come closer than any other researcher, even without publishing his valuable map. But even if the mystery of the Josephine de Martinique has been solved, the legend will survive, and the stories will be told of the men who spent, and sometimes gave, their lives for her gold.

CHAPTER 11

Charlie Steen and the Moab Uranium Boom

The engine in Charlie Steen's rickety old drilling rig sputtered and strained, as the bit gnawed ever so slowly into the red rock of Moab, Utah. Steen had sweated in the July sun for nearly three weeks, running the temperamental piece of machinery when he wasn't repairing it.

This wasn't just another hole, it was Steen's last chance to strike it big. There was no room for errors. He was out of money, and with a family to support he couldn't afford to be wrong about the claim he called Mi Vida.

The diamond bit had chewed its way down 197 feet through the sedimentary layers. As he drilled, Steen examined the cylindrical cores that came up. So far he had found only red rock on top and an unfamiliar soft, gray material at seventy-two feet. There was still no sign of the canary yellow, uranium-bearing carnotite he was after. Still his hopes remained high as he approached the two-hundred-foot mark, where he had predicted a valuable deposit of radioactive rock might be.

Suddenly the smoke-belching drill began to whine. The bit slowed down and, with a loud CRACK! snapped under the torque of the massive engine. Steen had faced setbacks—too many to count—but this was a big problem. The bit had sheared off deep underground, and there was no way to extract it.

Broke and discouraged, Steen got in his old jeep and headed back to the town of Cisco, trying to imagine what he would tell his mother, wife, and four children. After all, hadn't his family suffered enough? How much longer could they follow Charlie and his crazy dream around the Southwest, living meagerly in small trailers in the middle of nowhere, eating jackrabbits, crackers, and peanut butter?

With the bit broken off in the ground and no money left to begin another hole, Steen had given new meaning to the term *rock bottom*. As he drove those one hundred lonely miles from Mi Vida back to Cisco, he faced the fact that his days as a prospector were over. He would have to move back to Texas and get a job with an oil company, like the old one he hated so much. But deep inside he had no regrets about his effort. He knew that only people who face the worst failures can ever know the greatest rewards.

The first successful experiment in isolating radium earned Madame Curie the 1911 Nobel Prize, when scientists saw that the newly discovered element held much promise in the treatment of cancer and other applications. The extraction process required over four years of continuously boiling tons of pitchblende, a soft radioactive rock found in the mountains of Germany and Czechoslovakia. Curie needed an easier method of refining, so she began to search for a more pure source of radium. Her quest brought her to southern Utah in 1912. There she found copious amounts of bright yellow carnotite, an ideal source of uranium, another radioactive element.

Not long after Curie's visit, carnotite mines sprung up all over Colorado and the eastern half of Utah, an area geologists call the Colorado Plateau. By 1923 the area had become the world's largest supplier of uranium. But when deposits of much higher-grade ore were found in the Belgian Congo, and several other countries, mining and refining in the United States came to a grinding halt.

Charlie Steen, uranium king
UTAH HISTORICAL SOCIETY

It would take an act of war to revitalize the US quest for uranium, which came when the Japanese attacked Pearl Harbor in 1941. Suddenly there was an urgent need for domestically produced uranium for the construction of a new kind of weapon, one that only existed in theory.

Scientists around the world agreed on uranium's destructive potential, but a nuclear bomb had never been built. Under the utmost secrecy, the US government assembled a group of the best American scientists and engineers to develop the new superweapon. Time was of the essence.

With the mission code-named the "Manhattan Project," the team of technical experts was deployed to a main research lab in Los Alamos, New Mexico. Meanwhile geologists fanned out into Colorado and Utah, opening some of the old vanadium and radium mines from twenty years earlier.

By the summer of 1945, the scientists had built the first-ever nuclear bomb. After a test explosion in Alamogordo, New Mexico, World War II was ended with the August 6 bombing of Hiroshima, Japan, and the destruction of Nagasaki on August 9. Less than a year later, the government created the Atomic Energy Commission (AEC) to increase the US nuclear arsenal. The United States was at peace, but the Soviet Union and its allies now had nuclear weapons of their own, and within a few years a full-blown arms race was under way.

The AEC offered $10,000 incentives for prospectors who located uranium deposits, and it also provided money for building roads to the claims. Almost overnight Moab, Utah, went from barely more than a scenic watering hole along a dusty trail to a frenzied boomtown, bursting at its seams with prospectors and their dreams.

By 1949, twenty-eight-year-old Steen was a trained geologist whose work had taken him through the jungles of South America and over the windswept plains of the United States. He had more experience and education than the average prospector, and a bit of a cocky streak. After returning to school in Chicago for a master's degree, he moved to Houston with his new wife, M.L., and got a job as a geologist for Standard Oil.

Steen had some difficulty working for large companies. He liked to do things *his* way, which meant trying to be efficient and logical—two things not commonly found within big bureaucracies.

One day, while on the job, Steen let his temper get the best of him, and he was fired for "rebellion against authority" when he refused to fill out some redundant paperwork. From the experience he learned to respect the boss, but it was his "my way" attitude that would ultimately pay off for the eccentric rock hound.

Steen found himself at a crossroads. M.L. was pregnant with their fourth child, and Charlie needed to find work—but he wanted to be his own boss. The idea of prospecting for uranium sounded romantic and adventurous, if a bit risky. M.L. was nervous about it, but she had faith in her husband. If the odds could be in *anyone's* favor, it would be Charlie, given his background.

Compared to prospecting for gold, silver, or even oil, finding uranium deposits was easy, especially for those who used a machine called a Geiger counter. But the machines were only good for finding small deposits on or just below the surface. Steen didn't like the idea of using a Geiger counter. He considered himself a geologist first and prospector second. He studied rock formations and pored over geological maps of the Southwest. He didn't want to make a strike that would pay for a new car—he wanted to make history.

By the spring of 1950, Steen found himself in Dove Creek, Colorado, with his old jeep and trailer and a beat-up drilling rig. M.L. remained in Texas with the kids for couple of months before bringing them to Colorado, where locals were already snickering about the crazy uranium prospector who didn't use a Geiger counter. No one had attempted to drill for uranium, but Steen was going to show the skeptics that he wasn't just a gambler, but a good geologist.

Steen was just beginning to get acquainted with the area and still trying to find a "grubstake," or a person who would outfit a prospector with supplies, usually in exchange for a percentage of anything found. One of the first men he dealt with was Bill McCormick, a local store owner.

McCormick was hesitant to get involved with someone who didn't use a Geiger counter, but Steen convinced him he was an expert when it came to rocks and that he was willing to do the tiresome legwork. Without a formal contract the two partnered up, and McCormick took Steen to an area called Big Indian Wash, where they staked a number of claims. Without the resources to begin drilling, however, and fearing a harsh winter, the Steens loaded up the trailer and moved to lower country—a desolate area of southern Utah called Yellow Cat Wash.

As the Steens endured the cold winter, Charlie continued searching for a grubstake, while studying geological maps of the area drawn up by the AEC). He knew that small amounts of uranium had been taken from the Big Indian Wash area by the owners of fourteen claims, collectively called Big Buck. The ore from that mine was used for the Manhattan Project, but it was of low quality and the surrounding area was considered barren by the AEC.

Charlie believed higher-grade ore could lie just to the southwest of Big Buck, beneath a geological formation known as the Lisbon anticline. After asking permission from the Big Buck owners to look around behind their property, Steen staked out twelve claims on a few thousand square feet of unassuming red rock. He wrote his name on a piece of paper, as well as the Spanish names *Mi Vida, Mi*

Corazon, Pisco, and *Mi Alma,* among others, and put the paper in a tin can to protect it from the elements.

When Charlie went back to tell M.L. of his promising venture, he was met with terrible news: His mother, Rose, had suffered a heart attack in Houston. Charlie went to Texas to help Rose recover and returned to Utah two weeks later. He told M.L. that their plans for the new claims at Big Indian Wash would have to be put on hold. Rose had unpaid medical bills, and Charlie saw no other option than to move the family to Tucson, Arizona, where he could make steady money as a carpenter.

For the next year, while Charlie cut boards and hammered nails in the Arizona heat, his mind wandered to the twelve claims on the desolate red rock of Big Indian Wash. Even after receiving a few promising job offers in his old field of oil geology, Charlie kept his sights set on Utah. Finally the Steens returned to Utah, this time to the town of Cisco, but they were once again faced with hardship when M.L. got pneumonia. Finances dwindled as she recovered, and Charlie was having no luck in finding someone willing to invest in his Big Indian claims. After all, who would want to take a chance on a chunk of rock in the middle of a vast area that the AEC had considered "barren of possibilities"?

The Steens' luck finally began to turn when $100 checks began arriving every month from Rose, who had sold her Houston home. A short time later Rose showed up in Cisco, ready to roll up her sleeves and help her son out in any way she could while M.L. tended to the children. The two made a trip to Big Indian Wash, where Charlie's rocks and tin cans remained just as he had left them, marking the boundaries of his claims.

With financial help from Rose, Charlie was able to pay someone $500 to bull-doze a four-mile gravel track from the county road up to the claim. Then his old part-ner, McCormick, came to the rescue by lending Charlie a bigger and better drilling rig. In exchange for his assistance, Charlie promised McCor-mick a 49 percent share of any profits from the venture. The drilling equipment was a vast improvement over what Charlie had showed up with

Charlie Steen struck it rich not too far from this drilling rig at Big Indian Wash. UTAH HISTORICAL SOCIETY

in Colorado the previous year, but it still required a skillful hand to operate and repair.

On July 4, 1952, Charlie began drilling a bore hole at his Mi Vida claim. His goal was to hit a layer of rock called the Shinarump conglomerate, some two hundred feet down, past the Wingate and Morrison Formations. Over the next couple of weeks, he was delayed by a broken pump, worn-out drill bits, and other mechan-ical issues, all of which sapped his energy and drained his pocket-book. Now, more than ever, he needed to make a strike. It was either hit pay dirt or head back to Houston with his tail between his legs. The final discouraging blow came on July 18, when the whining engine snapped itself free from drill shaft, leaving the expensive bit lodged deep underground. There was no hope of retrieving it.

On the way back to Cisco, not ready to face his family with the news, Steen pulled his old jeep into a service station owned by his friend Buddy Cowger. Although he was bound to a wheelchair, Cowger was caught up in uranium fever and was excited to show off his brand-new Geiger counter to Steen. After telling Cowger about the bad news at the Mi Vida claim, Steen remembered that he had thrown a piece of the mysterious gray rock into the truck and went out to grab a chunk for Cowger to examine. Steen tossed the core sample on the table inside, where it came to rest against Cowger's new Geiger counter. The needle on the counter went crazy. Steen thought the device might be broken, but Cowger assured him it had already been used to look at ore samples, although none had been this pure!

The layer of rock Steen found seventy-two feet down was radioactive pitchblende, the same kind of soft rock that Madame Curie had used in her experiment! Since he was expecting yellow carnotite, Steen had forgotten all about pitchblende. Yet he knew right away that what he had, sitting there on Buddy Cowger's table, was more pure then the European version and would be highly desirable to the AEC. He also knew that his troubles were over. No more cold, cramped trailers. No more hungry kids. No more *bosses!* The Steen family would be rich. It was just a question of *how* rich—and how soon. To know the true potential of Mi Vida, Charlie needed more equipment and an investor with deeper pockets than McCormick.

During the excitement of any mining boom, there is always a way for con artists to make some quick cash. Steen was accused of "salting" his mine, or bringing in the high-grade ore from somewhere else, in order to convince investors it came out of Mi Vida. The controversy made it difficult for Steen to find money for the project. Even McCormick wanted out of the deal when his own "silent" financial partner became suspicious of Steen's discovery.

When the story of Mi Vida broke in the *Denver Post* on August 30, 1952, Steen got a phone call from one of his old bosses in Houston, William Hudson, now living in Casper. Steen told him that McCormick's share of the mine was up for sale, and Hudson became interested. With the help of another man named O'Laurie, the two bought McCormick's 49 percent for $15,000 and also loaned Steen an additional $30,000 to begin work at Mi Vida. In late October, Charlie had a lawyer draw up some papers, and the Utex Corporation was born.

Even amid all the excitement, Steen was still nervous. He was under more pressure than ever to prove that his hole in the ground would be profitable. Instead of drilling a second exploratory hole, a common and prudent approach, he once again put all his chips on the table and suggested they sink an expensive six-by-eight-foot shaft down to the layer of pitchblende.

It took two months of drilling, blasting, and "mucking," or removing the loosened rubble, while Steen and his partners crossed their fingers. Finally, on December 1, Charlie's thirty-first birthday, the work crew hit the gray pitchblende, at a depth of sixty-eight feet. The long, stressful wait was over. The skeptics had been silenced, and it was time to get on with the business at hand.

Charlie moved his family to Moab in early 1953, where they rented a modest three-bedroom duplex. There wasn't a house in town big enough, or extravagant enough, for Charlie. So within a few short months, he had his dream mansion built high up in the red rocks, just north of town.

Prior to building the mansion, however, Charlie splurged on something he had always wanted: a big, red Lincoln Town Car. When M.L. asked him for a new washing machine, he surprised her with a diamond instead. Still, diamonds can't clean clothes, so Charlie had the family's laundry flown to Grand Junction and back each week for cleaning. Such extravagances, however, were just a warm-up for what was about to come.

Steen cherished the free time his money allowed him even more than the material items he could now afford. He took his family on a seven-thousand-mile road trip in the Lincoln. He bought a Cessna airplane; hired an old college roommate, Pete Byrd, as his pilot; and flew to Salt Lake City or Denver for the simplest of errands. He flew to Baja, California, for fishing trips on his sixty-five-foot yacht named *Minnie Lee*, after his wife. Many trips were spontaneous. Once, after flying to Grand Junction for a business meeting, he outfitted his crew with new clothes and supplies and didn't return to Utah for thirty-eight days.

By now the national press had picked up Steen's incredible rags-to-riches story. His colorful personality made for great magazine and newspaper articles. He traveled the country giving speeches and making the occasional television appearance. The one thing, besides uranium, that Charlie and M.L. .became famous for were the lavish parties thrown at their hilltop mansion. Invitations went out to all kinds of prominent figures, including politicians and Hollywood icons like James Stewart, Henry Fonda, and Dorothy Malone.

Steen recognized the responsibility that came with having money, and his role as a philanthropist made him all the more likable. He donated huge sums to the improvement of Moab's infrastructure, building new churches and even a $50,000 hospital.

By the end of Mi Vida's first six months in operation, the mine had produced $1 million in ore. Around this time, a wealthy Texas businessman offered Steen $5 million for the mine. But Charlie knew he was on a winning horse, and it was still early in the race. He turned the Texan down, and later turned down even bigger offers.

Although he loved being king of the Moab uranium boom, Charlie was not content to simply get the ore out of the ground. He knew that the AEC refineries were having trouble keeping up with the growing number of mines, as well as the military's demand for uranium, so he started thinking about building his own mill. There were only a couple of mills in the country capable of extracting radioactive elements from rocks, and those mills were owned by the federal government.

Just like when he arrived in Moab with his drilling rig, people thought he was crazy. But after getting approval from the AEC, Charlie and a partner, Mitch Melich, got a $3.5 million loan from the Chemical Bank of New York and charged ahead to become the owners of the first private uranium mill in the United States. A partnership was created between Utex and a metallurgy company owned by Melich's father-in-law to form URECO, or the Uranium Reduction Company.

Unbeknownst to Steen and Melich, the AEC had also awarded a mill-building opportunity to the Ute Milling Company, owned by the large Atlas Corporation. Its owner, Floyd Odlum, from New

York, had deeper pockets and more connections in the industry than Steen did, and there wasn't room for two mills in the same area. Steen was furious. But in the end he realized that partnering up with Ute Milling would be better than not building a mill at all. So the two companies teamed up, and construction of the new facility, dubbed "the coffee grinder," was complete by October 1956.

Less than two years later, URECO was processing around 1,700 tons of ore per day and was the largest employer in Grand County. Steen was lauded by the Utah State Senate and publicly thanked for his accomplishments. It wasn't long before Steen's friends began encouraging him to run for public office. He would require a little "cleaning up," however, as Charlie was prone to blurting out the first thought that came to his mind, which isn't always the best trait for a politician.

After a campaign of handshaking and baby kissing, though, the charismatic and confident Steen won a seat in the Utah State Senate. He served on the Industry, Labor, Mines, and Taxation Committees but introduced several bills outside his area of expertise. One pet project was a push to ease Utah's strict liquor and gambling laws. His stance put him at odds with the Mormon majority, and he made little headway in his efforts.

In early 1961, fed up with Utah's conservative politics and the challenges he faced as an outsider, Steen resigned from the Senate. He moved the family to Reno, Nevada, where he bought three ranches with plans to breed Arabian horses.

About a year after the move, Charlie and his partners sold most of their Utex shares to the Atlas Corporation. Charlie received some $10.5 million over the next four years, yet the Uranium King didn't seem to know what the word *retire* meant. Mining was in his blood now, and he kept his hands in many different ventures, anticipating the next big strike.

Some of his investments included gold and silver mines in the United States and abroad, a marble quarry, and a few oil and gas prospects. He invested in Nevada real estate and had a large cattle herd, as well as two dozen Arabian horses. While his attempts to diversify his investments seemed wise, Steen was addicted to high-risk ventures, many of which didn't pan out. He lost $3.5 million in an aircraft company that went out of business. He sunk $700,000 into an orange grove that never produced. He put $250,000 into a gourmet pickle factory, but the cucumber crops froze two years in a row.

Not deterred by the spate of bad luck, Charlie, M.L., and the kids moved into a 27,000-square-foot mansion outside of Reno that made their Moab house look like a shack. It took three years to build and was christened with one of Steen's signature blowout bashes.

All parties must come to an end, however, and Steen's high-flying lifestyle spiraled down to earth in February 1968, when six men from the Internal Revenue Service came to the ranch and confiscated some of the Steens' most valuable belongings. The Steens were charged with owing almost $2 million in taxes. It seems that Charlie made some illegal tax deductions involving some of his unsuccessful business ventures. He was also accused of failing to report a capital gains tax for his sale of Utex stock. Besides the taxes owed to the IRS, Steen had racked up close to $5 million in other debts. His yacht was repossessed by the government, as well as his three twin-engine planes and office building.

The man who could once borrow almost any amount of money from any bank in the world was now buried under an avalanche of unpaid bills, his credit destroyed. After pawning the beautiful jewelry he had bought for M.L. and filing for Chapter 11 bankruptcy, he barely managed to save the house from foreclosure.

Steen spent the next four years trying to make a comeback in the mining business, but his name was not enough to reclaim his former status. To make matters worse, he sustained a severe head injury while operating a piece of drilling equipment at a copper mine in California. The blood clot in his brain almost killed him, and it took almost a year to recover his ability to speak. Behind on the bills again, the Steens were evicted from their Reno mansion in 1974.

Through all the hard times, the marriage of Charlie and M.L. remained the one happy constant. On more than one occasion he credited his own success to having her by his side. M.L.'s death in 1997 left the Uranium King alone for the next nine years. Charlie remained poor until the day he died of Alzheimer's disease in 2006.

CHAPTER 12

The Ghosts of Heritage Park

August 11, 1847, was a warm, beautiful day in the Salt Lake Valley. The Thirlkill family had completed their tiresome cross-country pilgrimage only three days earlier, and after a short rest they had begun to explore the area. While cooling off at City Creek, three-year-old Milton was left unattended for a few moments, and the curious boy made his way to some slippery rocks at the water's edge. Playing too close to the water, he lost his footing and the current yanked him away before he had a chance to scream. His small body was recovered in a pool downstream.

The happiness shared by the pioneers had, for the Thirlkills, suddenly vanished. They had come so far and been provided for. Now they had been called to give up a child.

Milton was buried near downtown Salt Lake City, on a piece of land at 360 South and 200 West. Over the next few years, thirty-two other pioneers were interred at the same location, which was also part of an ancient tribal burial mound. The Mormon remains had been long forgotten until they, along with the American Indian bones, were discovered in 1986 when construction crews excavated the area.

Not wanting to waste valuable space in the heart of the commercial district, city planners chose to exhume the remains and

Brigham Young's Forest Farmhouse now sits on Heritage Park property, about two miles from its original location near Salt Lake City.
MICHAEL O'REILLY

transfer them to the Pioneer Trail State Park, now known as This Is the Place Heritage Park. The name comes from the famous words uttered by Brigham Young when he first laid eyes on the Salt Lake Valley in 1847.

The bodies of the Mormon pioneers were moved to a small cemetery outside a mock village, which had been established for the benefit of tourists wanting to get a feel for the way things used to be. After a traditional burial ceremony, the Indian remains were moved from the downtown location and placed in a concrete tomb, also on park property.

Heritage Park now consists of relocated buildings such as Brigham Young's Forest Farmhouse and replicas of other famous historical places, including the Cedar City Tithing Office and the

Atkin, Kimball, and Rich homes. Over the years, however, visitors to the historical park have reported strange vibes, unexplained wackiness, and paranormal phenomena, including actual encounters with ghosts. Like young Milton Thirlkill, many of those buried in Pioneer Cemetery were children, and sometimes, usually late at night, their high-pitched laughs (screams?) can still be heard near the graveyard.

Brian Westover, a blacksmith and tour guide at Heritage Park, told a story of a strange occurrence at Pioneer Cemetery during one of the park's haunted Halloween events. Actors were posted at several of the buildings to scare the daylights out of people who paid to get scared. A woman and young boy were in the cemetery—she acting like a grieving mother and he the spirit of a dead child. But while the woman was sitting up against the fence, she distinctly felt a hand stroke across her face. She spun around, swatting at what she thought was a friend trying to spook her. She got spooked all right, because no one was around but her son running through the tombstones, some twenty yards away. It was at that point she decided maybe it wasn't a good idea to play "haunted cemetery" in a graveyard that needed no help with the act.

A few of the other locations used for the haunted Halloween event were later said to have been visited by ghosts, according to witnesses. Westover said that one explanation for the increased paranormal activity might involve the spirits' being disrespected by the mock performances.

Surprisingly the most commonly witnessed and talked-about apparition haunting Heritage Park is not a resident of Pioneer Cemetery, but the ghost of Ann Eliza Young, the nineteenth wife of Brigham Young. Many believe Ann Eliza's spirit still haunts the very house where she spent so many unhappy years of her life. One of only two women to get divorced from Young, Ann Eliza went on to record a lucid and revealing biography titled *Wife No. 19: The Story of a Life in Bondage.*

After the Youngs moved out of Forest Farm, as it had been called, the house was bought and sold several times over the years, before being donated to the Latter-day Saints (LDS) Church, who then traded it to the State of Utah. In 1975 the structure was moved several miles from the Sugarhouse area to Heritage Park, on Salt Lake City's east side.

These days Heritage Park is staffed by a grounds crew and a group of tour guides, who, rumor has it, have kept a journal detailing many of the park's strange occurrences. Although most visitors probably don't know much about Ann Eliza Young, or have no idea what she looked like, there is an uncanny consistency to the descriptions of her ghost. People tell of witnessing a woman in a long, dark gown standing in the window of one of the house's second-level rooms.

The ghost of Ann Eliza has been seen both at night and during the day. One particularly unnerving incident involved a tour guide who swears that while showing a group of people a framed photograph of Ann Eliza, the image mysteriously lifted itself from the wall and floated out, toward the shocked observers, before receding back into the frame.

So why, if Ann Eliza disliked her home and her husband so much, would she wish to spend her afterlife haunting the Forest Farmhouse? We may never know the answer to that question, but we do know a few things about the house itself. Brigham Young owned several houses, and Forest Farm was a place none of Young's fifty-one wives ever wanted to go. To be "sent to the farm" meant they had fallen out of favor with Young and were relegated to endless hours of hard work in the fields.

Ann Eliza was twenty-four when she married Young in 1868. Five years later she filed for divorce, citing neglect and cruelty on Brigham's behalf. By that time Ann Eliza had traveled to the East Coast, and after observing some of the ladies on that side of the country, felt that Utah's women were not keeping up with progress of women elsewhere. Upon her return to Utah, she could not help but voice her opinion to those around her. After only a year of marriage, the headstrong "wife number nineteen" was outcast as an agitator and sent to the Forest Farmhouse.

Ann Eliza never liked Forest Farm in the first place. She complained to Brigham, who designed much of the home himself, that the walls were thin, making it too hot in the summer and too cold in the winter. Another gripe she had was the location of the stairs leading to the second floor. In order to reach the upstairs bedrooms, people, including hired help, were required to walk through the dining room and the parlor.

When Young eventually built Ann Eliza her own house near downtown, she was insulted by the fact that its staircase was also located in the parlor. Some who claim to have seen Ann Eliza's ghost at the relocated farmhouse say they saw her standing at the top of the same staircase she hated so much.

Ann Eliza's biography is very interesting, but books can only get you so far when you're trying to learn about ghosts. I needed to know more about the haunted buildings of Heritage Park and, if possible, meet Ann Eliza herself. My timing couldn't have been better. The first day I met with Brian Westover, he gave me a lot of information about the park's ghostly residents. But he said if I really wanted to have a chance of seeing the ghost of Ann Eliza, I should return the next night, when the Paranormal Investigation Team (PIT) of Utah would be on the property.

"You mean, like the Ghostbusters?" I asked with a little laugh. Now I know he has a sense of humor, but Brian didn't crack a smile. He had *seen* them. He had *heard* them late at night, as he made the rounds, locking up the old buildings alone in the dark. Not only that, but he had recorded every paranormal encounter he had experienced or heard about since he began working at the park a few years earlier.

He told me about one incident that occurred while he was in the Andrus house with several members of a paranormal team from Salt Lake City, called the Ghost Office. Upon entering the house and going up the stairs to the second level, Brian noticed two things. The first thing was the abnormally cool temperature of the room. It was a hot August evening, and normally the second level of the Andrus home was stuffy, to say the least. Yet Brian was almost shivering.

The second thing he noticed was a strong smell of urine, which seemed to come and go. They had been inside only a few minutes when a female member of the team felt something tug at her ponytail. Sensing it may have been a ghost, she quickly said, "Do that again, you're welcome to pull my hair if you're trying to get our attention." But nothing happened with her hair.

"As this was going on," Brian said, "all of a sudden, downstairs the front door opened and footsteps walked across the floor . . . I had always thought if I heard a ghost it would be this very creepy, stealthy kind of creaking sound, and it wasn't, it was just very businesslike, is the only way I can describe it . . . It never even occurred to me that it might be a paranormal incident. I thought, well it must be security, or someone from the park. We went downstairs, and no one was there. Both the doors were closed and locked from the inside. All four of us heard it as clear as can be."

The story got my attention, as did another one of Brian's personal accounts from the same home. He was working in the home some years ago, and he went upstairs to get something from one of the closets. As he got to the second floor, he could hear several people talking in one of the rooms on that level. "I could not make out what they were saying, but it was definitely voices. Of course there was nobody in the home but me."

There are other scary stories from the Andrus home, which Brian says is probably the most "active" building on the property. That may be so, but I was dying to . . . rather, I was *hoping* to catch a glimpse of Ann Eliza, so I asked Brian for a few stories about Brigham Young's Forest Farmhouse. I quickly found out that I should be prepared to meet more than just Eliza, if I was still brave enough to join the paranormal team late the next evening.

After Young sold the Forest Farmhouse, but before it was moved to Heritage Park, it was used as a church. One night, a man who had just committed a robbery and killed somebody in the process broke into the house and hid in the cellar. Authorities later killed the robber, and his ghost makes occasional appearances to this day. An apparition resembling Brigham Young himself is also seen, as are the ghosts of Sara Decker Young and Brigham's favorite son, John A. Young.

Other paranormal mischief in the Forest Farmhouse include the unexplainable scent of baking bread, the spontaneous extinguishment of candles, items falling from the mantle, and the mysterious migration of objects from one part of the house to another.

I was curious as to what kind of techniques the paranormal team would employ to document any spirits or strange occurrences. Brian educated me on the use of EMF, or electromagnetic field devices, which measure a type of energy in the vicinity. The theory is that if a spirit is in a room, it will draw energy from the area. Such phenomena are said to be responsible for drops in temperature, as Brian experienced in the Andrus home, as well as the draining of both disposable and rechargeable batteries.

Video cameras are also used, but generally not with as much success as audio-recording devices. When using a tape recorder in a spiritually active environment, the goal is to capture electronic voice phenomena, or EVP, snippets. Usually a person will simply leave the device in the record mode for the duration of the session and carefully listen to the tape later. Occasionally an entity will manifest itself on the tape with a sound of some kind. Often the EVP is a very human-sounding voice, and other times it's just a strange sound. In most cases the sound left on the recording is completely inaudible to the people present at the time it is made.

Then there's perhaps the most important and valuable piece of equipment: the human being. Any good ghost-hunting team should have at least one person with some level of clairvoyance, telepathy, or other extrasensory perception. When I met the para-normals the next night, I quickly figured out who that person was.

None of PIT's four members, Leslie Larson, Carrie Pytlik, Lance Lukesh, and founder Mike Zimmer, had ever been into the Forest Farmhouse. Perhaps more important, none of them knew anything about the home. Now I don't have ESP, but I could sense that Carrie was sensing something. There was something different about her. We stood in the front room of the oddly symmetrical farmhouse and exchanged introductions, keeping our voices low. It was pitch dark, about ten at night. *Are these people trying to scare me?*

Lance is the technical expert of PIT, having worked on infra-red and night-vision camera systems during a twelve-year stint in the Air Force. I asked him where his interest in the paranormal originated. "I had quite a few experiences when I was younger," he told me. "The house that got me into all of this was spooky—it's still spooky. Some people can be disbelievers all their lives, until they walk into that certain place and go 'this is different.'"

Lance said he didn't feel psychic or clairvoyant as a child but said, "As far as feeling sensitive to things, I'm kind of working on that right now . . . I think everybody has it to a degree. Now, whether they listen to it or not, it's totally up to them."

After hearing Brian talk about the technical side of ghost hunting, I wanted to know what kind of gear Lance was plan-ning to use to help me catch a glimpse of Ann Eliza. He felt as if even the most high-tech cameras on the market were still a ways behind the curve in terms of observing the supernatural or para-normal. "The equipment we use, none of it was designed for this, so we have to compensate for that. It's designed to pick up a solid object, and we're not dealing with that. We're trying to think way outside the box now."

How far outside the box is Lance trying go? "I'm a big fan of the electromagnetic spectrum," he said. "When you're dealing with the ultraviolet, and infrared, and all the wavelengths that are within the electromagnetic spectrum, just what we're seeing can't be all there is. Our eyes only see certain frequencies, and it's such a narrow band of frequencies within the spectrum."

What was the point of all of this? What did the team plan on doing with any video or EVPs they did happen to record? Where the heck is Ann Eliza?

"We would plan to come back and try to focus on whatever we were getting the most activity on," Mike said, "and see if we can identify a person. If we can identify a person, we try to do a little research on that person and find out what they're doing here, why they haven't crossed over to the other side. I think we've probably done that a time or two . . . It would be nice to help somebody and answer some of our own curiosities about what's going on."

At this point in the conversation, I heard Carrie say that she smelled something cooking. The rest of us could not smell anything but the musty aroma of antiques and old rugs. Again, Carrie said she detected a strong scent of baking bread and possibly something frying in a pan. She also claimed she had a "bad feeling" about one of the two staircases leading to the second floor.

Baking bread, the staircase Ann Eliza despised . . . *I knew I had a feeling about Carrie!* I felt like my chances of seeing Ann Eliza were getting better just by having Carrie around. I was happy to hear from Mike that 99 percent of the ghosts he's dealt with have been benign: "We don't even know that we're dealing with 'ghosts' in the traditional sense. Chances are since people have been saying these are ghosts for thousands of years, they're probably ghosts, but I have no idea. I've never seen one . . . Carrie, have you?"

"Uh, yeah," Carrie offered sheepishly, while looking around as if distracted by something. *Maybe Ann Eliza finally showed up.* "A lot of people will misunderstand a possible ghost. A ghost can be mischievous, just annoying, or trying to get your attention." Carrie's voice trailed off as she wandered into another room, possibly following the scent of baking bread. I overheard her say to Leslie that she was "getting a feeling" about a certain area.

Although I remained optimistic about seeing Ann Eliza's ghost, I didn't want to hinder the efforts of PIT, who seemed to know what they were doing just fine without having me bumbling around in the dark, asking them silly questions.

I called Brian a few days later to find out what went on in the farmhouse after I left. Nothing happened at the farmhouse, although the team leader, Mike, reportedly saw what he called a "luminescent ecto-apparition" on the stairs of the Kimball home. The phenomenon was seen with the naked eye but not caught on camera. "It's only the second time in ten years that he's actually seen one of these things," Brian said. "They want to come back and do some more work."

Good. I'll be there. And hopefully Ann Eliza will be too. Perhaps she can sign my copy of her book. It's a great read, but I've never seen someone get so mad about a staircase.

CHAPTER 13

Bigfoot in the Beehive State?

One night in 1980, Utah residents watching the six o'clock news were surprised by a report of multiple Bigfoot sightings in a North Ogden suburb. The owner of a trout pond in nearby Coldwater Canyon claimed to have seen the tall, hairy creature nonchalantly plucking fish from the shallow pool. A man living near the mouth of the canyon said his chickens were killed, and another man lost several sheep and pigs to the hungry Bigfoot.

The dense vegetation along the creek at the bottom of the canyon seemed like the perfect route for an elusive critter to travel unnoticed, yet hikers and landowners continued to spot Bigfoot over the next seventeen years.

There have been and probably always will be skeptics, but for a few North Ogden residents the vivid memories of their experiences have made them believers. One Salt Lake City resident, Darrell Smith, who passed away in 2012, said in a 2008 interview, "Everybody who lives at the bottom of Coldwater Canyon knows about Bigfoot 'cause he's been in their backyard. It's kind of hard to see one and then not believe in it." Clearly though, it is possible to believe in Bigfoot without ever seeing one, because the Ogden sightings changed Smith forever.

Over three decades, Smith collected more than two hundred firsthand stories from almost as many people. Although Smith never laid eyes on the hairy beast, he was never discouraged from the quest to prove Bigfoot's existence.

Success in Bigfoot hunting is largely a state of mind, and much of the satisfaction lies in the pursuit. There are tangible rewards, of course: fresh air, nice views, camaraderie, and fitness. Years of roaming Utah's rugged landscape left Smith strong and spry until Lou Gehrig's disease took its toll.

Many people who are accustomed to hearing tales of Bigfoot, or Sasquatch, that originate in the Pacific Northwest of the United States and Canada have no idea how old and widespread the legend really is. He has been called different things on different continents all over the world for hundreds, perhaps thousands, of years.

Yeti has been spotted in the mountains of Nepal and Tibet. *Yowie* is the name given to him by the people of Australia. Residents of mainland China refer to him as *Yeren*, while the Lakota Indians of North America call him *Chiye-tanka*, or "Big Brother." In Southeast Asia, where the lower jawbones and teeth of a huge, apelike mammal have been found, Bigfoot has acquired the Latinized scientific moniker *Gigantopithecus blacki*.

But what about Utah? Is it realistic to think Bigfoot could thrive or even survive in the Beehive State? "Any species' range is dependent upon suitable habitat," said world-renowned Bigfoot expert Jeff Meldrum of Idaho State University, in an interview conducted via e-mail. "There is ample habitat to support a large omnivore in eastern Utah, especially in the Uintahs, the Wasatch, and the Colorado Plateau. Reports of eyewitness encounters and footprints generally occur in those regions."

A true scientist, Meldrum cares little about making the six o'clock news, or even convincing the public that Bigfoot is real. "That will only happen if or when a specimen is secured." No, he wants to unravel the biological mystery by answering one simple question: Is there a large unrecognized primate behind the legend of Sasquatch?

Where exactly is Bigfoot on the evolutionary scale? Smith didn't think we are simply dealing with a new species of primate. He was certain that Bigfoot has a humanlike nose, which distinguishes him from anything inhabiting the earth today, besides *Homo sapiens*. In addition, there is no species of monkey, gorilla, or ape that walks exclusively on two feet the way Bigfoot does.

Although Smith was enthusiastic about his pursuit of Sasquatch, he lacked the scientific background and credentials of Meldrum. Unfortunately for Meldrum, he himself endures a certain degree of intellectual isolation within the academic world, where few people support his efforts and even fewer share his beliefs. "It is a challenge of making a case that the evidence at hand warrants serious consideration," he said.

While Meldrum has spent years giving "serious consideration" to oversize plaster castings and odd hair samples, it's tough for the professor to find other scientists willing to follow in his (Big) footsteps. When Meldrum comes across an unidentifiable piece of hair, for instance, his excitement is tempered by professional pragmatism, but he won't let anyone tell him it *didn't* come from Bigfoot. And why should he? Of course speculation is the enemy

Jeff Meldrum has one of the largest collections of Bigfoot print castings in the world.

PAUL HOSEFROS

of scientific procedure, and while Meldrum argues that he's only trying to keep an open mind, others continue to refuse to believe in something they've never seen walking around—or dead.

Even while swimming against the academic and scientific current of detractors and critics, Meldrum remains positive, hoping the tide will turn and bring with it a new respect for those who study secretive creatures, also referred to as cryptozoology. He has managed to make a few allies, if not outright converts. "Prominent naturalists, conservationists, anthropologists, and so on have spoken in support of the need to take a serious look at this evidence," he said. Then he gave his old foes a reprieve. "Some in the media are beginning to deal with the question in a more objective fashion."

Meldrum addressed the most common question asked of Bigfoot hunters and skeptics alike: Why has a dead body never been produced? How is it possible, for example, that a Bigfoot has never been killed by a car? "If this is a species of large primate," Meldrum said, "then its intelligence is at least on par with that of a chimp or gorilla, perhaps greater. Given its rarity and its solitary habits, it is not surprising that they avoid traffic."

If Meldrum is right about the lack of Bigfoot roadkill, it seems logical to extrapolate the "intelligent recluse" theory outward to account for the complete lack of a single Bigfoot carcass or body part in North America. But Darrell Smith had a different explanation. "We know that Bigfoot buries its dead. They've been seen burying their dead. A couple guys in California saw two Bigfoot burying a third. . . . The guys went back to town to get help, 'cause they wanted to dig it up, but when they returned they couldn't remember where it was."

Besides the teeth of *Gigantopithecus*, the most common kind of "hard evidence" we have of his existence are the thousands of plaster castings, or molds, taken from footprints found in soft soil. Smith has three such castings, although his are different from the typical five-toed tracks found in most places. The tracks he found have three toes, which makes him believe he may have discovered a new kind of Bigfoot, perhaps one of reptilian origin.

Smith had difficulty getting other Bigfoot hunters to back him up with the idea of a three-toed Bigfoot, especially Meldrum, who has collected over two hundred plaster footprint castings—all of which have five toes.

"I've been trying to convince Meldrum for several years that there are three-toed ones, as well," Smith complained. "He can't accept that. I never used to believe it myself, either. All the tracks I saw up on Hoyt Peak had three toes."

During a 2008 interview, Smith picked up the sixteen-inch-long three-toed chunk of plaster and examined the specimen intensely, as if he might at that moment discover a previously unnoticed hair or scale or pattern of dermal ridges. "I've never seen what makes these tracks. This might not even be Bigfoot . . ." Smith's voice trailed off as he pondered the possibilities.

Given his knowledge of extraterrestrial beings, and of the animals in the Utah area, Smith had no other choice but to come to the conclusion that if the tracks were reptilian, they were most likely from outer space. There was a brief internal struggle, as if he wanted to maintain the division between his alien and Bigfoot interests, but he could not, for the evidence was right in his hands. And with how little is known about Bigfoot, who can really say for sure that the mythical hairy beasts are not descended from alien reptiles?

Smith understood, however, that in the world of cryptozoology one must pick one's battles carefully. While he was proud of his three-toed casting, he wasn't in a hurry to cause any rifts in the tight-knit community of Bigfoot researchers. "People who have seen Bigfoot and know Bigfoot's real, they'll say, 'Reptilians? No way.'" Really, one couldn't blame him for not wanting to sound crazy.

Every one of the two hundred or so Bigfoot stories Smith has been told is recorded on a three-by-five card, and, although he seemed to know most of the stories off the top of his head, the cards came in handy when he gave lectures at Bigfoot conventions. Each story belongs to a corresponding red foot-shaped sticker on a large map of Utah that Smith kept in his basement. Virtually covered in little red feet, the map denoted sighting locations in every canyon from Monticello to Morgan, and on every mountain from Vernal to Wendover. "And that doesn't even include what you can find on the Internet," Smith said with a grin.

Looking back down at his stack of cards, Smith's bright blue eyes lit up, as he recited one story after another. A close friend had found a fossilized Bigfoot skull on top of Lone Peak. An entire troop of Boy Scouts and their scoutmasters watched a large hairy creature for half an hour. He had been spotted by hunters, fishermen, campers, Forest Service workers . . . Smith was prepared to recite each of the two hundred stories, if not for the author's interruptions.

When Smith interviewed people to get their testimonies, he could tell they were telling the truth by the visible impact the experience has had on them. "It might have been twenty years ago, and they get scared all over again. I know of one guy, for example, he saw one [Bigfoot] above Logan, running across the top of a ridge. He saw it as a kid, and it scared him really bad, and when he tells the story to this day, you can almost see tears coming down his face."

Smith and Meldrum shared an interest in Bigfoot, but that's where the similarities ended. Smith liked to hear and tell stories, while Meldrum deals in well-reasoned hypotheses tied to hard evidence. Clearly their approaches and beliefs are wildly divergent, which seems to be a fundamental problem among Sasquatch researchers.

For Meldrum, a rigorous scientific approach is the only way to make any sort of discovery in the field of cryptozoology. "As with any community of people," he says, "there are often diverse opinions on a variety of subjects . . . Are they [Sasquatch] more apelike or more humanlike? Are they paranormal or associated with UFOs? Is there a government or industry conspiracy to hide their existence? Some of these opinions are based on very little or very unreliable evidence, if any at all." Clearly Meldrum feels that such speculative deviation from facts and evidence only creates setbacks in the learning process, while at the same time damages any credibility cryptozoologists might have with other researchers and the general public.

Smith said that many Bigfoot are spotted by motorists—people like his friend, Ron, who had an incredible experience while driving up Farmington Canyon with his wife and children. After rounding a tight corner in a densely wooded area, Ron slammed on the brakes to avoid hitting something tall and hairy standing in the middle of the road. For at least five minutes, the giant beast stood there on the centerline, looking around as if he couldn't decide where to go. Finally he started moving, and for a moment the entire family was on edge as the beast walked toward the car, swinging his long arms. A few strides later he was past them and out of sight. Ignoring his wife, who begged him to keep driving, Ron jumped out of the car to get a better look at the creature.

When he opened the door, everyone inside was hit by a blast of foul-smelling air, which is a trait Bigfoot are known for. "When they are putting out a smell," Smith said, "whether it's on purpose or not, a lot of people have said it's like rotten meat, or the worst smell they've ever smelled. But then I've been within feet of them [Bigfoot] and never smelled a thing. I've had them follow me through the woods and walk around my camp."

While there may not be any record of a Bigfoot being killed by a car, Smith said that more than one has been shot by a human. But they are tough to bring down. He related a story supposedly told by Teddy Roosevelt, in which two miners shot and wounded a Bigfoot near their camp. Later the creature returned and killed one of the miners. Roosevelt himself reported hearing the strange call of an unidentifiable animal one night while camping in the Rockies. He also had an encounter with an animal he was positive was not a bear, but that was very large and stood on its hind legs.

Perhaps the most amazing story of a Bigfoot shooting comes from the Texas panhandle in 1976. Smith said a high-ranking Air Force official told him about three Vietnam veterans who were out late at night hunting for bobcats and coyotes when they came across a dark lump in a clearing. All three of them fired upon what they thought was a bear, which suddenly stood up on two legs and ran a short distance. The men all fired again, knocking the animal down briefly before it sprang up again. As the creature made its way to into the thick brush, the men each got off a third shot. They were confident whatever it was they shot couldn't be lying far away. Yet the size of the animal was enough for them to take some caution, and they decided to return the next morning.

The following day the hunters picked up a blood trail and followed it a short distance into the prickly thicket of cactus and mesquite. Not taking any chances, the man in front proceeded slowly and was armed with a .44 magnum handgun. Suddenly a huge female Bigfoot came crashing through the brush toward them. Three shots from the .44 rang out, and the creature went down, shaking the ground upon impact. The men couldn't believe their eyes when they noticed the humanlike face of the animal. A short time later they found her mate, the male they had shot the night before. "These guys thought they had murdered a couple of primitive human beings," Smith said. "Human eyes, human nose, human teeth. They're huge, and they're heavy and covered with hair, and they're naked, but they're *people*. So they decided to bury them and never talk about it to each other or anybody else."

Over the years, however, the men started thinking more and more that perhaps they hadn't shot a human at all, but a Bigfoot. Certainly they couldn't be charged with a crime, so they came forward and told their story on the radio and in the newspapers.

Smith was convinced that Bigfoot has a sense of humor. "They like to play with you," he said. "I don't think they ever intend on hurting anybody." Then another story popped into his head, this time his own memory of a trip into the Uintahs with a friend. "It was late at night, and we were just sitting around the campfire when we heard a stick break behind us. Thirty seconds later we hear a stick break over here [moving his hand in a circle around himself]. Every thirty seconds or so a stick would break. For five straight hours until three in the morning he was breaking sticks around our camp.

"They'll throw rocks all around you, but not at you. They'll break sticks, they'll do lots of different things to play with you. Sometimes when you're on the trail that they're on and they don't want you there, they'll just reach over and pull out a thirty-foot aspen right out of the ground and lay it across the trail . . . stack them up like a fence."

Not everyone who has crossed paths with a Bigfoot has had great things to say about him. In his book *The Wilderness Hunter*, Theodore Roosevelt tells a story about an old frontiersman named Baumen, who told a riveting tale about a friend of his who was killed by a mysterious beast.

According to Roosevelt, who was not a dishonest man himself, Baumen was very convincing when he said that the two men had been stalked for several days as they ran traplines in the Rocky Mountain wilderness.

The trappers had stuck together for days, frightened by the nighttime grunts and growls of the creature lurking beyond the flickering shadows of their campfire. Finally on the day they were about to leave, they had separated only a short time when Baumen returned to find his partner's dead body with a broken neck and several puncture wounds to his throat. The tracks Baumen found were not those of a bear or mountain lion, but something that had approached the site and departed on only two feet.

Bigfoot has made his way into the mythology of so many different cultures that one of two statements must be true: He either exists, or human beings have a certain need and desire for him to exist. Why else would there be so many sightings?

Is it possible that, between all the jokers and hoaxes and the tall tales and unconfirmed accounts, the entire Sasquatch debate has simply grown tiresome for the average person? Has such "Bigfoot fatigue" worn people out to the point that they've sided with the skeptics, essentially by default? Is seeing really the only way to believe?

If you never lay eyes on Bigfoot in your entire life, what would it take for you to think he's real? A track? Perhaps an eerie, unidentifiable moaning in the woods outside your tent late at night?

If Sasquatch really exists, he is no doubt secretive. And he must also be a little sad. For no sound in the world could be more lonely than Bigfoot's call followed by the desperate silence of his waiting for a mate's reply—a mate so many people don't believe in.

CHAPTER 14

UFOs and Aliens in Utah

The wide-open skies of the western United States have long been a hotbed for UFO sightings and stories of all things alien, beginning with the supposed 1947 crash of a flying saucer in Roswell, New Mexico. Perhaps it is merely coincidence that the same part of the country is home to all kinds of aviation research and design, some of it top-secret.

Utah has played an important role in the development of things that fly high, move fast, and go "boom." High-tech weapons are tested at the Dugway Proving Grounds, jet-powered cars scream across the salt flats, and space shuttle booster rockets roar to life at the Alliant Techsystem development center in Promontory, north of Salt Lake City.

Some claim not only to have seen spacecrafts, but to have been abducted and experimented upon or even impregnated by one of three types of aliens: "grays," "greens," or "reptilians." The most common alien theory involves these beings, who have not only visited Earth but inhabit our planet, both on the surface and underground. It is important to draw the distinction between the belief in aliens and belief in UFOs. Many UFO witnesses aren't convinced they've seen alien crafts, but they explain their sightings as government tests involving classified military technology.

"Alien" Dave Rosenfeld: always ready for an encounter
MICHAEL O'REILLY

Adding to the speculation of such projects is the mystery surrounding the Air Force's secret "Area 51" base, which lies within
the Nevada Test and Training Range.

At first I was reluctant to include a chapter in this book about
aliens and UFOs. I knew there would be a lot of information and a
lot of sightings and descriptions of spacecraft and little green men.
I struggled with a way to bring such accounts together in an interesting way. Then I met "Alien" Dave Rosenfeld.

It wasn't hard to spot Alien Dave's truck at the MUFON
meeting. MUFON stands for "Mutual UFO Network." A huge
sticker on the vehicle advertised the Utah UFO Hunters Investigation Team (UUFOH), a group Dave started in 1996. And
although the Ford Bronco's camouflage paint job may have come

in handy for alien encounters, it didn't help it blend in among the shiny sedans and SUVs in the library parking lot. It was obvious he was serious about aliens.

Inside the library I found a group of fifteen people in a meeting room, including Alien Dave, who was wearing a pair of camouflage pants. He began the meeting by describing an incident that had occurred just two weeks earlier in central Utah. A friend called him and said he had found a set of strange tracks in the snow outside his trailer. When Dave arrived at the scene, he was shocked to discover that the tracks began in the middle of an undisturbed field of snow, as if the creature had simply descended from the sky.

As the two of them photographed the long, three-toed tracks, Dave noticed a small, thin piece of a skin-like substance about the size of a half-dollar. After carefully removing the piece from inside the track, it was delivered to another friend, who had a high-powered microscope. He sliced off a sliver of the specimen and placed it on a slide for examination. When he applied a small drop of solution to the sample, the cells appeared to come to life, moving around and dividing right before their eyes. It still was not clear to them what they were dealing with, but they believed the skin (or whatever it was) must have come from something living. By the looks of the tracks, it seemed to be reptilian. And when was the last time anyone had seen a large reptile in Utah? In the winter?

Thinking they might be closer than ever to proving the existence of reptilian aliens, Dave and his friend shaved off another small piece of the skin sample and sent it to the Federal Bureau of Investigation for DNA testing. Several days later, without any explanation, the FBI returned the sample and Dave's $450 check.

Determined to identify the creature that left the skin, or at least confirm that the creature is not from Earth, Dave plans on taking the sample elsewhere for DNA testing.

The incident wasn't Dave's first experience with a reptilian. Some years ago he and his girlfriend were waiting for a plane in the Denver airport when a strange feeling came over him as he looked toward the corner of the terminal. "I just had a feeling that something was over there," Dave said. "So I thought in my mind, mostly just messing around, I thought 'You know, I *see* you.'"

And that's when it happened. An odd-looking creature about eight feet tall stepped right out of the wall, holding its chin up proudly, flashing a bright array of orange and green color. "It said back to me, in my mind, 'Yeah, take a good look,' and then it stepped back into the wall. . . . I looked at my girlfriend and said, 'Did you see that?' And she said, 'See what?' And I said, 'Aw nothin.'"

For the next hour or so, Dave paid close attention to the same corner, and the other walls, hoping to catch another glimpse of the reptilian creature. "It was an experience where you're seeing something that's not human. It was very beautiful at the same time. I didn't feel any evil coming off of it." The story was one of many strange tales I was about to hear.

Dave related one particular Utah incident that resembled a modern-day Roswell cover-up. One night a few years ago, a UUFOH team member we'll call "Sarah" was working at the Pizza Hut in Fort Duchesne when she received a phone call from a friend who said some type of circular craft with flashing lights had been seen flitting about over the town. Sarah didn't take the call too seriously; her friends were known for prank calling her at work. But then she got another call from a different person who saw the same thing. Finally a third person called and reported that not only had he seen the UFO, but the craft may have crash-landed just outside of town.

No sooner did Sarah hang up the phone than she made out the wail of police sirens in the distance, growing louder as she sped out the front door. Main Street flashed like a blue and red fireworks display as a group of five police cars accompanied by a low-flying helicopter raced in Sarah's direction, and past her.

What puzzled her most to see were the vehicles following the sheriff: several black Suburbans, a flatbed semitrailer, and a few more police cruisers, including some from the local Indian reservation. The convoy was headed toward a dirt road leading out of town—the same road Sarah's sister lived on.

Immediately Sarah became suspicious of the black Suburbans, because she knew her small town's police department did not drive such vehicles. She ran back inside and made a quick phone call. Her sister answered and said the lawmen were driving by her house as they spoke.

It seemed strange to both girls that the unmarked Suburbans happened to be in the area just moments after the UFO sightings occurred. After all, they must have come from Salt Lake City, over an hour away.

"Whoever these people were in the black Suburbans," Dave said, "they either had previous knowledge . . . or there is some kind of 'black' covert operation going on in Fort Duchesne, and they were already there."

Sarah drove to her sister's house and was there only thirty minutes when the procession of vehicles came speeding back toward town. The two girls noticed that the same flatbed semi-trailer they had seen before was now hauling something concealed behind tall fabric panels.

A few days later Sarah ran into the sheriff in a coffee shop. He was a man she had known for years, so she figured he would be honest with her if she asked about the incident. "It was a suicide," the sheriff said, clearly avoiding the subject. Not satisfied with his answer, and puzzled by his shifty mannerisms, she prodded him further. His response was to the point. "Just leave it alone, Sarah," he said before walking out the door.

One MUFON member, Sharon, who lived in a trailer home on eighty acres of property in southern Utah, shared one of several

This image was captured by Dave Rosenfeld in Utah's Canyon of Dreams.
© 1998–2008 DAVE ROSENFELD, UTAH UFO HUNTERS;
WWW.ALIENDAVE.COM

firsthand UFO experiences. One night while stargazing in the yard, she sensed that one of the heavenly lights was giving her a signal. She thought it might be some kind of extraterrestrial life-form. "I said, 'Well come on down, come visit.' And this blue light came and just shot over the trailer and stopped. The puppies were dead quiet, and the cats were just having fits."

Suddenly Sharon heard a loud knock on the back door, which surprised her, because the trailer's door was four feet off the ground with no stairway or porch. "Historically you're told if it comes to the back door, you don't open the door. If it had come to the front door, I would have opened the door. So I didn't open it."

Then she saw the bright blue orb zoom toward the west before it stopped and came speeding back, crashing against the side of the trailer, shaking it almost off of its jacks. After it rocked the trailer a second time, Sharon became frightened. But she knew she had to stand her ground. "I just told it, 'You cannot come here, you cannot be here because you did not come in the right way.'"

The blue light retreated back up into space, where Sharon watched it until the morning light reclaimed the sky. When she went out to look for tracks in the deep snow near the back door, she found nothing—nothing, that is, except a large dent in the door.

"I felt that it was a negative energy," she said. "Had I thought it was coming in love or trust, I would have answered the door. I'm used to living with ghosts and things. I'm psychic, and I'm used to that, but this was a bad energy."

What could possibly have made a dent in her back door without leaving any tracks in the snow? What kind of alien force would approach an isolated trailer with such aggression, yet be driven off by a lone woman?

The monthly MUFON meetings are a support group of sorts, and no one laughs at or discounts the stories of any member. Which was good for me, because I had a story of my own to tell.

It was 1994, and I was having the best summer a nineteen-year-old could ask for. I was traveling the United States, competing in mountain bike races and roaming vast stretches of highway that seemed as endless as the freedom of youth. I had the chance to explore obscure, out-of-the-way towns like Wendover, a mini–Las Vegas that straddles the Utah-Nevada border.

There isn't much to explore in Wendover, especially when you're not old enough to lose all your money in the casinos. So when I got to the neon oasis, I kept driving until I was enveloped once again by the quiet darkness of the desert. Almost completely void of humans, the five-hundred-mile triangle between Salt Lake City, Las Vegas, and Reno is one of the areas in the United States least affected by the "light pollution" that brightens more-populated states.

Having put about seven hundred miles on the old Toyota that day, I searched for a four-by-four trail that would take me off the interstate a fair distance. After turning off on a promising two-track, I followed the bumpy route up to the top of a small hill—a perfect spot to throw down my sleeping bag.

I traveled light in those days, with no use for a tent. And who would want to blot out the stars in one of the darkest spots in the country? As I lay in my sleeping bag, admiring the celestial display, I looked westward and noticed two lights rising from the horizon miles away. I took them to be airplanes, possibly fighter jets, which I knew were common in those parts.

The two lights continued to rise together slowly, as if flying in formation. Suddenly they both stopped and abruptly changed direction. They did the same maneuver again, completing a Z-shaped pattern in the sky. Then, as if jerked by a cosmic tether, both lights quickly zipped off into space, disappearing at a rate of speed that seemed impossible for any kind of fighter jet.

What had I seen out there in the desert? A plane? A spaceship? Had I just spent too many hours behind the wheel? I don't know, but I could not identify the flying object, which officially makes it a UFO sighting.

Regardless of what others think about my experience, whether or not they believe me, I am tremendously thankful for having seen the UFO, or pair of UFOs. Because I know I'm not crazy or delusional, my experience allows me to take seriously the accounts of others and to hear their stories with an open mind, without passing judgment. The stories of the late Darrell Smith required at least that much of their listeners.

Before he passed away in 2012, Smith attended MUFON meetings for over fifteen years, and he was proud to be involved with such a diverse group. In a 2008 interview, he said, "Through the years we've had nuclear physicists, doctors, lawyers—people of all occupations and educations. . . . Even retired military people tell stories, so in a group you'll have a thousand times the information you'd find on your own."

Smith was Utah's resident Bigfoot expert, but when he wasn't searching the dirt and snow for Sasquatch tracks, he turned his eyes to the stars. "You'd be surprised at all the UFO stuff that's happened right over this [Salt Lake] valley. Black triangles, saucers, little funny-looking people who aren't quite human. . . . There are people in the group who have had experiences with aliens on the ground." According to Smith, the Pentagon has admitted that fifty-seven different types of aliens have visited our planet. I could not confirm this claim.

Writers such as Zecharia Sitchin and David Icke have done much to nudge the once-obscure fields of "alternative science" and "alternative history" in the direction of mainstream culture. They have had a major impact on the way Smith looks at the world. "The more I read Zecharia Sitchin," he said, "the more I think maybe there are aliens all over the place, especially reptilian shape-shifters. I think some of them are people we know."

Philip Schneider, a popular figure in alien culture, had for years told wild tales of fierce battles between grays, greens, and reptilians unfolding beneath us, in a series of tunnels and bases that spans the entire United States.

Schneider claimed that, while working as a government-contracted geologist, he was involved with the construction of 131 bases, each over a mile down. He said that when the military originally tried to establish subterranean bases in the Southwest, they confronted reptilian beings who had been maintaining their own bases for perhaps thousands of years. What ensued was a turf war that continues today.

Not only had Schneider seen aliens, but during one encounter in Dulce, New Mexico, he was attacked by two angry grays attempting to defend one of their own bases. He was able to stop both of them with well-placed shots from his 9mm handgun, but not before one of the grays fired a blue laser beam into Schneider's stomach. He was severely wounded and his hand permanently disfigured.

A few years later, in 1996, Schneider was mysteriously murdered. Many believe he was killed because he came forward with a series of speeches and a tell-all video revealing the top-secret tunnel and base projects.

During the hours I spent at the MUFON meeting I heard many stories, some of which were hearsay, and some of which were firsthand accounts. The group covered a wide range of topics related to aliens and the unexplained, and it became clear that such meetings are not just a place where conspiracy theories take root, but where they multiply, morph, and thrive. Are there really reptilian aliens living among us, who use their shape-shifting capabilities to appear human? Could it be that powerful world leaders and politicians are actually reptilian aliens who operate within secrets societies like the Illuminati and the Freemasons? Is it possible that the white contrails behind certain airplanes are not actually water vapor but toxic *chemtrails* sprayed by the government as a method of population control? I may not spend a lot of time trying to find the answers, but I was happy to engage in an open-minded discussion about it with interesting folks like Alien Dave and Darrell Smith.

If it is true, as some have suggested, that the reptilians have infiltrated human society in order to facilitate the creation of a New World Order, is it possible they also have influence among Mormon leaders? Given the secretive nature of the Latter-day Saints (LDS) Church, the idea is compelling.

But there actually is a piece of Mormon doctrine whose origins are quite cosmic. In 1835 Joseph Smith was presented with a scroll found in ancient Egypt and asked to do his best to decipher the strange foreign writing within. What he came up with was the Book of Abraham, a text that came to have great importance to followers of the Mormon faith because it revealed the origins of mankind on Earth. Smith's translation can be found in the *Pearl of Great Price*, a five-part book containing other influential scriptures, sections of which are taken from the New Testament.

According to Smith's translation it all began on a distant star, sometimes referred to as the planet Kolob. The scripture describes how Abraham (of the Old Testament, also shared by Jews and Christians) "saw the stars, that they were very great, and that one of them was nearest unto the throne of God . . . and the name of the great one is Kolob." (Book of Abraham 3:2-3)

The Egyptian scrolls also contained three hypocephaluses, or disk-shaped artifacts engraved with elaborate hieroglyphics, one of which was interpreted by Smith as "Kolob, signifying the first creation, nearest to the celestial, or the residence of God." (Book of Abraham, Facsimile 2, Figure #1 explanation)

The translation also tells of a time in the future, when the Earth, Moon, and Sun are properly aligned "one planet above another, until thou come nigh unto Kolob, which Kolob is after the reckoning of the Lord's time; which Kolob is set nigh unto the throne of God, to govern all those planets which belong to the same order as that upon which thou standest." (Book of Abraham 3:4-9)

So what does all of this mean? Assuming Smith translated correctly, we still cannot be sure the message was intended to be interpreted literally, or figuratively, the way other scriptures use stories, or allegories, to teach a lesson about human behavior.

Just as Muslims might disagree on how to interpret the Koran, and Jews might disagree on how to read the Torah, Mormons are divided on how exactly to interpret the Book of Abraham and the Book of Mormon. For most members of the LDS Church, the important thing is the overall message of the faith, not whether or not God once lived on a distant planet or star called Kolob.

And why should it matter? Like many other religious teachings, the story of Kolob sure makes for an interesting read— almost as interesting as the tale of reptilian aliens who roam the secret tunnels far below Salt Lake City and zip through the sky in flying saucers.

BIBLIOGRAPHY

Arave, Lynn. "Grave Robber Desecrated up to 300 Sites around 1860." *Deseret News*, December 2, 1991.

Bailey, Lynn. *The Search for Lopez: Utah's Greatest Manhunt.* Tucson, AZ: Westernlore Press, 1990.

Boren, Kerry Ross, and Lisa Lee. *The Gold of Carre-Shinob.* Springville, UT: Bonneville Books, 1998.

Brooks, George R., ed. *Jedediah S. Smith: His Personal Account of the Journey to California 1826–27.* Glendale, AZ: Arthur H. Clark Company, 1977.

Cannon, Anthony. *Popular Beliefs and Superstitions from Utah.* Salt Lake City: University of Utah Press, 1984.

Cordell, Linda. *Archaeology of the Southwest.* 2nd ed. Walnut Creek, CA: Left Coast Press, 1997.

Denton, Sally. *American Massacre: The Tragedy at Mountain Meadows*, September 1857. New York: Vintage Press, 2003.

Devitry-Smith, John. "The Saint and the Grave Robber." *BYU Studies Quarterly* 33, no. 1 (1993).

Dunning, Linda. *Specters in Doorways: History & Hauntings of Utah*. Alton, IL: Whitechapel Productions Press, 2003.

Fleek, Sherman. "The Mormon Trail Played an Integral Role in the Westward Push and the Settlement of the West." *Wild West*, June 1997.

Gunnerson, James H. "Plains-Promontory Relationships." *American Antiquity* 22, no. 1 (1956): 69–72.

———. "Plateau Shoshonean Prehistory: A Suggested Reconstruction," *American Antiquity* 28, no. 1 (1962): 41–45.

Hafen, Leroy R., and Ann W. *Handcarts to Zion*. Lincoln: University of Nebraska Press, 1960.

Hill, William. *The Mormon Trail*. Logan: Utah State University Press, 1996.

Kantner, John. *Ancient Puebloan Southwest*. Cambridge, UK: Cambridge University Press, 2004.

Meldrum, Jeff. *Sasquatch: Legend Meets Science*. New York: Tom Doherty Associates, 2006.

Morgan, Dale L. *Jedediah Smith and the Opening of the West*. Lincoln: University of Nebraska Press, 1953.

Newell, Maxine. *Charlie Steen's Mi Vida*. Moab, UT: Moab's Printing Place, 1996.

Parr, Ryan, Shawn Carlyle, and Dennis O'Rourke. "Ancient DNA Analysis of Fremont Amerindians of the Great Salt Lake

Wetlands." *American Journal of Physical Anthropology* 99, no. 4 (1996): 507–18.

Pierce, Norman C. *The Dream Mine Story*. Salt Lake City, UT: self-published, 1958, 1972.

Pointer, Larry. *In Search of Butch Cassidy*. Norman: University of Oklahoma Press, 1977.

Rhoades, Gale R. *Footprints in the Wilderness: A History of the Lost Rhoades Mines*. Salt Lake City, UT: Dream Garden Press, 1971.

Ringholz, Raye C. *Uranium Frenzy: Saga of the Nuclear West*. Logan: Utah State University Press, 2002.

Roosevelt, Theodore. *The Wilderness Hunter*. Upper Saddle River, NJ: Literature House, 1970.

Rutter, Michael. *Outlaw Tales of Utah*. Guilford, CT: Globe Pequot Press, 2003.

———. *Myths and Mysteries of the Old West*. New York: MJF Books, 2005.

Saitta, Dean, and Randall McQuire. "Although They Have Petty Captains, They Obey Them Badly: The Dialectics of Prehispanic Western Pueblo Social Organization." *American Antiquity* 61, no. 2 (1996): 197–216.

Shaffer, Stephen B. *Out of the Dust*. Springville, UT: Council Press, 2005.

Stegner, Wallace. *The Gathering of Zion*. New York: McGraw-Hill, 1964.

Taylor, Troy. "The Ghost of The Great Salt Lake—Or The Legend of John Baptiste." Accessed February 1, 2017. http://www.prairieghosts.com/baptiste.html.

Thompson, George A. *Lost Treasures on the Old Spanish Trail*. Salt Lake City, UT: Western Epics, 1999.

Wharton, Gayen, and Tom Wharton. *It Happened in Utah*. Guilford, CT: Globe Pequot Press, 2007.

Young, Ann Eliza, *Wife No.19: The Story of a Life in Bondage*. Hartford, CT: Dustin, Gilman, 1876.

Young, Brigham. Journal entry, January 27, 1862, LDS church archives, 341–42.

INDEX

About the Author

Michael O'Reilly is an artist, writer, and business owner. He holds a master's degree in poetry from the University of Utah and resides with his wife and two children in his home state of Michigan.